SpringerBriefs in Computer Science

Series Editors

Stan Zdonik
Peng Ning
Shashi Shekhar
Jonathan Katz
Xindong Wu
Lakhmi C. Jain
David Padua
Xuemin Shen
Borko Furht
V.S. Subrahmanian
Martial Hebert
Katsushi Ikeuchi
Bruno Siciliano

For further volumes:
http://www.springer.com/series/10028

Sibel Adali

Modeling Trust Context
in Networks

 Springer

Sibel Adali
Rensselaer Polytechnic Institute
Troy, NY, USA

ISSN 2191-5768   ISSN 2191-5776 (electronic)
ISBN 978-1-4614-7030-4   ISBN 978-1-4614-7031-1 (eBook)
DOI 10.1007/978-1-4614-7031-1
Springer New York Heidelberg Dordrecht London

Library of Congress Control Number: 2013935126

© The Author(s) 2013
This work is subject to copyright. All rights are reserved by the Publisher, whether the whole or part of the material is concerned, specifically the rights of translation, reprinting, reuse of illustrations, recitation, broadcasting, reproduction on microfilms or in any other physical way, and transmission or information storage and retrieval, electronic adaptation, computer software, or by similar or dissimilar methodology now known or hereafter developed. Exempted from this legal reservation are brief excerpts in connection with reviews or scholarly analysis or material supplied specifically for the purpose of being entered and executed on a computer system, for exclusive use by the purchaser of the work. Duplication of this publication or parts thereof is permitted only under the provisions of the Copyright Law of the Publisher's location, in its current version, and permission for use must always be obtained from Springer. Permissions for use may be obtained through RightsLink at the Copyright Clearance Center. Violations are liable to prosecution under the respective Copyright Law.
The use of general descriptive names, registered names, trademarks, service marks, etc. in this publication does not imply, even in the absence of a specific statement, that such names are exempt from the relevant protective laws and regulations and therefore free for general use.
While the advice and information in this book are believed to be true and accurate at the date of publication, neither the authors nor the editors nor the publisher can accept any legal responsibility for any errors or omissions that may be made. The publisher makes no warranty, express or implied, with respect to the material contained herein.

Printed on acid-free paper

Springer is part of Springer Science+Business Media (www.springer.com)

Contents

Chapter 1
Introduction

We make complex decisions every day, requiring trust in many different entities for different reasons. How are these decisions made? They are not made by combinining many single trust evaluations in isolation. Many interlocking factors play a role, each impacting others in a dynamic fashion. To study trust in decision making, we must first develop a system level view of trust. By this, we do not mean the study of trust beliefs, but the study of how different beliefs are all combined into an evaluation of trust for complex goals. This is what we aim to achieve in this brief. We view trust evaluation as a continuous process, incorporating many different considerations that play a role in the final decision. We define **the trust context** as the system level description of how the trust evaluation process unfolds. We review what is known about this system, and how it impacts the design decisions for computational trust models.

As an example, let's assume that Alice wants to buy the original cookbook written by Julia Child, called "Mastering the Art of French Cooking" from a used book seller through Amazon's marketplace. First, she realizes that there are multiple editions of this book, with different numbers of volumes, by different publishers. To disambiguate, she first collects information by reading reviews of different versions, and scans other online information sources to understand the differences between the various editions of the book. Based on this information, she decides how desirable each version of the book is, and matches the different editions to the copies offered by different sellers. Soon she discovers that the information provided by the sellers is also somewhat vague. She uses clues she obtained from the reviews to make sure a specific book being sold is the version she wants the most. Furthermore, she needs to take into account the sale history of the sellers to decide which one seems to be the best choice at the right price point for the reported condition of the book. Finally, the purchase is made.

In fact, the seemingly simple decision of buying a book involved the consideration of many parameters collected from different sources. Along the way, Alice had to make many different trust decisions. She had to trust that the information provided by the reviews was correct, coming from reviewers that she did not know. Sometimes, she used a simple rule for determining the reliability of the reviews: if

S. Adali, *Modeling Trust Context in Networks*, SpringerBriefs in Computer Science, DOI 10.1007/978-1-4614-7031-1_1, © The Author(s) 2013

they were quite detailed, it was likely that the reviewers were knowledgeable about the review topic. She also had to trust herself in matching the desired book to the given descriptions. She had to trust that the seller was truthful in his description of the book, and that the seller was able and ready to fulfill her purchase.

So, Alice trusted many different people (and entities) for this one decision: the search engine used to find information about the book, the review writers, the seller, the Amazon marketplace, and herself. In addition, she had different goals in mind: the correctness of information, the ability of review writers to describe the book properly, the seller's trustworthiness in delivering the book, the ability of Amazon to collect and to present information about sellers, and the ability to resolve possible future problems. Finally, many outside factors may have impacted her decisions. For example, the first review she read was praising a specific version of the book. This review established a baseline for her and she evaluated everything else in relation to this version. She was not even aware that this was happening.

This is an example of how many decisions inherently require trust. Computing trust is not a simple matter of deciding whether someone or something is trusted or not. Decision making may involve complex goals made up of multiple sub-goals considered together, each requiring a trust evaluation for a different entity. Interdependent subgoals or even outside factors may affect the evaluation of trust. Furthermore, trusting Amazon, trusting the seller, and trusting online reviews may involve different considerations. Alice may rely on Amazon's reputation system to judge the seller, Bob, since she has not bought anything else from him before. However, Alice has experience with Amazon and can draw from her experience there. When judging information, her familiarity with the subject matter may play a big role in her trust evaluation. For example, if she already knows something about a specific version of the book, she can use it to judge the credibility of different reviewers. Based on the same information, she can even use it to form judgments about the websites hosting the reviews as to whether they are objective or not.

All in all, trust evaluation is complex because there are so many different criteria to take into consideration. These criteria are intricately connected to each other, and their evaluation is not instantaneous and not independent. Trust computation is even more complex in networks that combine people with each other through computational tools. With the increasing integration of computerized tools into everyday life and the increasing population of "digital natives" (the generation born after the digital age), the field of computer science is becoming even more ubiquitous. Today's computing is networked: people, information and computing infrastructure are linked to each other. The networked world is a part of almost all type of human activity, supporting and shaping it. Social networks connect people and organizations throughout the globe in cooperative and competitive activities. Information is created and consumed at a global scale. Systems, devices, and sensors create and process data, manage physical systems and participate in interactions with other entities: people, and systems alike.

These interdependent systems are sometimes called **socio-technological networks**. From now on, we will refer to these systems simply as networks. Many applications in these networks aim to assist people in making decisions and provide trustable tools and recommendations. However, these systems also rely on people for their operation and must take into account trust in their operation. They must trust that human input is correct, timely and unbiased. They must trust that human actions are sound. As a result, two different aspects of trust, algorithmic and human trust, exist together in networks and depend on each other in many ways.

The dynamics of these socio-technological networks go beyond what has been traditionally studied by social or cognitive psychology and modeled by computer science algorithms. Leading universities are forming new academic centers dedicated to the study of such networks in all their complexity. In this brief, we introduce the vocabulary necessary to study trust in socio-technological networks in a principled way. We define **trust context** as an independent concept and define its main components. We claim that the trust context describes how the trust evaluation is dependent on other entities and gives us the first step towards a study of trust in complex networks.

1.1 Organization of This Brief

The expected audience of this brief is network and computer scientists who study and model trust, and develop tools to compute trust. However, we are especially interested in trust computation that has a social or cognitive component. The broad review of trust offered in this brief is likely to be of use to researchers and practitioners in many other fields and help define a common vocabulary across different disciplines.

In Chap. 2, we give a definition of trust and provide the vocabulary necessary to study trust context in networks. In particular, we would like to define who is trusting whom for what, which signals are used to judge trust and how these signals are combined. The chapter introduces the readers to the notion of trust context as the encapsulation of the trust evaluation process.

We then introduce a survey of social psychology research in Chap. 3, with a specific emphasis on different network contexts that impact the trust evaluation. We also survey cognitive psychology research that explains how trust beliefs are formed and evaluated. We include related research in information trust and credibility to further show the difference in evaluating trust for information and for actions, two different contexts. We especially concentrate on some recent work in these fields that has not yet percolated into the computer science discussion and models. The social and cognitive psychology research that is often used as a reference in computational models seems to draw from a somewhat limited pool. Furthermore, some computational models make assumptions that are somewhat ad-hoc, not verified in experimental studies. Our hope is to infuse a broad perspective into this discussion by introducing some new perspectives in thinking about trust, and point researchers to the different lines of research in social and cognitive psychology.

In Chap. 4, we conduct a short survey of trust in the computing literature, where many different definitions of trust seem to co-exist. This survey does not go into details of any specific computational model of trust, but highlights how various definitions of trust can be mapped to the concepts we have laid out. The survey provides a multidisciplinary view of trust in networks, and different computational approaches to the study of trust. We also draw some parallels between social and cognitive science research and computing research.

Finally, in Chap. 5, we provide a summary based on the surveys in Chaps. 3 and 4. We describe some important contextual components of trust and how trust evaluation is impacted by these components. We make some modeling suggestions for future work.

1.2 Thanks

I am particularly thankful to the Army Research Laboratory for the establishment of the interdisciplinary Network Science Cooperative Technology Alliance (NS-CTA, ns-cta.org) and to Boleslaw Szymanski for incorporating my research into the vision of the Social and Cognitive Academic Research Center (SCNARC, scnarc.rpi.edu), funded as part of NS-CTA. The work that seeded this brief was funded as part of NS-CTA. I am also very thankful to colleagues that I have collaborated and had discussions with on this topic: Malik Magdon-Ismail, Mark Goldberg, John O'Donovan, Kevin Chan, Jin-Hee Cho, Andrea Krausman, Wayne Gray, Dakshi Agrawal, Munindar Singh, Jennifer Golbeck and Jason Kurusovich. Discussions with them were especially crucial in understanding the rich tapestry of research in trust as well as the various similarities and differences in discipline specific approaches. They also pointed me to relevant research in their fields when necessary. I wish to thank in particular William Wallace, Jennifer Mangels and Brian Uzzi for the in-depth conversations about trust. These conversations were not only extremely fun, but also fundamental to the evolution of this work. They pushed me to look at this problem from a broad perspective and challenged my thinking continuously.

I am grateful to my parents and my sister, who have always been a source of unconditional support and inspiration. Many thanks to Aaron Hertzmann who provided the illustrations for this brief. I hope they will both entertain and get the readers to think outside of the box in many different concepts. Aaron of course can later choose to publish the Cartoon Guide to Trust, which I think will probably explain the material better. Apparently, he does not need computers to produce compelling graphics.

And finally Rich, my trusted partner in science, that I dedicate this book to. You have been there with me at every step of the evolution of this brief. You provided valuable commentary as I filled the house with countless numbers of books with the same title and forced you to read some really rough drafts, always with a smile. You and I trust each other to . . ., well you know. I have a paper that describes the construct.

Chapter 2
Trust as a Computational Concept

Trust is a frequently used concept in many disciplines. In social sciences, the emphasis is on understanding how trust impacts the way people make decisions. The computing literature concentrates on the design of tools that can assist people in various tasks. Often these tools operate on a given model of trust and provide methods to measure trust in a specific application context. Before we go into the details of any such model or discuss the differences between different models, we first provide a broad definition of trust.

Fig. 2.1 Trust relationship between trustor and trustee

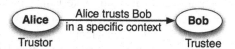

Trust is a relationship between a **trustor**, who we call Alice, and a **trustee**, who we call Bob (Fig. 2.1). Trust represents the trustor's willingness to be vulnerable under conditions of risk and interdependence [16]. Trust is not a behavior (e.g., cooperation) or a choice (e.g., taking a risk), but an underlying psychological belief that allows the trustor to put herself in a situation where she can be hurt or harmed by the trustee if her trust turns out to be misplaced. Trust is not a property of the trustor such as her propensity to trust. Nor is it a property of the trustee, such as his trustworthiness. Trust is a relationship between the trustor and the trustee that can be symmetric or asymmetric. Generally, the trustor trusts the trustee. The value of trust is either a quantitative or a qualitative measure that is used to check whether the trust relationship exists or to compare trust for different choices.

Regardless of the underlying model of trust, its value depends on the context. How much Alice trusts Bob depends on the underlying goal. For example, Alice trusts Siri on her iPhone to recommend her a good mechanic but not to choose a doctor. Why is this? The trust evaluation involves two different contexts: choosing a mechanic vs. choosing a doctor, which leads to two different evaluations. Furthermore, Alice's trust for Bob for the same goal at different times may vary based on external factors such as the existence of another information source. Hence, trust is not a fixed value between two entities. It is a function of the trustor, the trustee and the context. What is in this context?

To understand the elements of context, we need to examine what factors impact the trust relationship between two entities. Going back to the example of whether Alice trusts Siri to find a doctor, Alice's goal is to find a good doctor. The criterion considered in determining trust could be the expertise of Siri on the given topic, i.e., health. The reason that Alice does not trust Siri for choosing a doctor could be that she does not yet think of Siri as an expert in the topic of health. However, Alice's needs in this topic may go beyond expertise. Does Siri know enough about what Alice looks for when searching for a good doctor? Maybe Alice cares greatly about the doctor's bedside manner. Can Siri account for this appropriately?

An important factor in deciding to choose Siri for such a recommendation could be the underlying intent behind Siri's operation. Is Siri built to help people or to promote certain information sources based on monetary considerations? In other words, does Alice believe that Siri has good intentions towards its user? Alice may not have firsthand information to arrive at a decision on this topic and may instead consider it as an Apple product. She might love Apple and trust that Apple products are built with users' needs in mind. As a result, she might believe in Siri's good intentions as an Apple product.

Alice's goal may be more complex than just getting a doctor recommendation. She might not have a problem with getting doctor recommendations from Siri as a way of generating an initial list and then sifting through them herself. She also thinks that she can send some names to her friends and get their opinion. The contextual component of a decision involving trust incorporates both the goals and the dependencies inherent in these goals: Alice's dependence on the intelligent agent, on the entity/company that produced it, on herself and on her friends.

Most trust modeling work does not explicitly mention the context of a trust evaluation because it is generally implied by the specific domain the work is originating from. While some complex models implicitly incorporate some elements of context, there is no explicit effort in this area. As we will see, different theories may apply when considering dependence on different entities and different goals.

2.1 An Example of Different Trust Contexts

The issue of context is quickly becoming very important due to increasingly sophisticated networks that combine social systems with computational systems. As a running example, we consider the newly emerging field of **co-robotics** (Fig. 2.2), which is dedicated to the development and use of robots that work beside, or cooperatively with, people. This field provides us with many interesting examples of trust from very different contexts. All of these different types of trust must be addressed in the design of the new generation of robots.

Consider a robot that is designed to help people construct buildings by providing physical support and help. How can the person trust the robot?

Fig. 2.2 Trust in co-robotics, humans and robots working side by side

- First, if the robot is meant to understand natural language and take commands from a human operator, its capacity to understand language correctly is an important component. The person needs to be able to trust that the robot will understand the commands given to it. The robot's ability to assess its current state by sensing its environment are crucial considerations as well.
- Second, if the robot is giving information to the person, the person has to trust this information to be able to use it in decision making. Hence, the robot's ability to use information gathered from different sensors in problem solving are relevant to deciding whether to trust the robot or not.
- Third, the robot should be able to accomplish tasks, such as grabbing objects properly, lifting and positioning as needed.
- The first aspect describes the sensing ability of the robot, the second aspect involves its problem solving ability and the third aspect refers to the physical ability of the robot. These aspects of capability are not sufficient to "trust" the robot for a specific action. The person needs to believe that the robot is designed in such a way that it will not cause bodily harm (by accidentally bumping into people, for example). This involves not only the robot's capability, but also a person's beliefs about the intentions behind its design.

Let us now look at the situation from the robot's perspective. The robot also has to trust the human team member in various ways.

- When should the robot follow the person's commands? Does the person know what he is talking about? What if the command will hurt the person or is based on an unsound move?
- If the robot is cooperating with the person, it has to take into account that people are not always as careful as robots. What if the person is not paying attention? What if he is getting tired? What if he will not be able to hold a heavy part in place?

Some of these issues are explored as part of trust in automation. What if the person trusts the robot blindly and stops monitoring it? It may happen that the robot can signal that it is experiencing a serious malfunction, but this may not register with the human team member. Unfortunately, grave consequences of this problem have been encountered in aviation.

As the human and robot work together, they evaluate their trust and calibrate their actions accordingly. This is called learning to work together. In a social context, this is how each team member learns the intentions of the others and builds relationships. For effective teamwork, the person needs to trust the robot for accomplishing tasks, as well as for providing correct and timely information. The robot needs to trust the person to be capable of completing the tasks he is taking on, giving correct information and reacting to problems in a timely way so as not to endanger others. These definitions correspond to many different trust contexts. They imply different goals, dependencies and in some cases, cognitive processes. The aim of this brief is to explain and categorize these differences. In the remainder of this chapter, we provide an overview of the distinctions before going into a review of the literature in this area. First, we describe networks and the new interdependencies introduced by them.

2.2 Trust Context in Networks

Networks, especially socio-technological networks, bring the additional element of interdependence. When the human and robot are working together, there is no additional network context. However, in many realistic scenarios, the actions of a person are constrained by the network environment in which they are embedded. In many cases, the network provides new resources and enables people to take actions that they cannot take alone. For example, social constructs help explain how people in the same network can benefit from the existing social relationships in that network. Social networks allow people to come together and accomplish bigger tasks than they can accomplish alone. The individuals trust one another within the context of a specific network that they are part of (see Fig. 2.3).

In networks, the social relationships are only part of the story. Technology allows people to interact with many other people that are not part of their social network, but still contribute to create value for themselves and others. Many tools and services continuously depend on human input in one way or another. Wikipedia uses human contributors and editors to create and curate data. Amazon Turk and other crowdsourcing systems allow people to come together to solve problems. In these systems, the participation is either voluntary or paid, changing the motivation of the participants. Any service that relies on human input has to incorporate methods to assess when and if such input can be trusted and how to process the input depending on the level of trust. In addition to the motivation of the participants, one has to consider the issues of bias and noise in the human input.

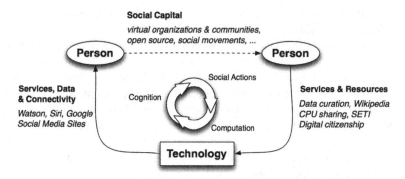

Fig. 2.3 Socio-technological networks introduce dependencies between people, dependencies of technology on human input, and human dependencies on tools provided by technology. All of these dependencies co-exist simultaneously in networks

Technology also relies on people to supply services to the network. In the case of CPU sharing systems like SETI@Home, the accessibility and reliability of computer systems are important concerns. Furthermore, systems and network security rely heavily on people abiding by protocols and implementing the necessary protection mechanisms. Similar to public health, networks remain healthy if the majority of its citizens are diligent about patching systems against vulnerabilities. In short, technology provides many sophisticated systems by trusting people to provide quality data, and secure and available systems.

These systems and services provided by technology are in turn used by people as resources in many daily activities. Many such services are of the type we just described: they rely on information created by people. IBM's Watson system used many sophisticated algorithms, analysis of past contestant behavior, and data sources like Wikipedia to answer Jeopardy questions better than any human contestant. Google relies heavily on the link structure of Web pages created by human input as well as the click behavior (pages people choose to click from those returned as answers to their queries). Social media sites depend heavily on user activity to decide which pieces of information and which users are prominent at a point in time. All these resources provide new capabilities to people, allowing them to find information and to connect with other people. People are also constrained by what these tools allow them to do. People trust these tools to get information and to accomplish tasks.

In summary, the networks provide context for trust relationships. People trust each other within a specific network. Socio-technological networks allow for new types of communities to form by online interactions. As a multi-faceted concept, trust is studied from many perspectives, such as social psychology, cognitive psychology, and computer science, among many others.

Some research addresses how communication mediated by technology is different than face to face communication. It is important to understand how people trust other people online. An equally important problem is how people trust information they find online. Finally, researchers study how people trust systems that they use for information or assistance.

Computer science studies how systems can make use of human input for many different services. There are many algorithms that incorporate a notion of trust, either implicitly or explicitly, to accomplish this. These algorithms often need to consider both social and cognitive aspects that impact people's decisions. As a result, understanding trust from these aspects is crucial to the development of principled algorithms, which is what we tackle in the next chapter. We then follow it with a review of trust in computing. However, we note that the study of trust in networks must incorporate not only an understanding of trust in each field, but also the dependencies between all the different components.

2.3 Defining Trust in Its Context

In the introduction, we defined the trust context as the system level description of trust evaluation. In particular, the trust context incorporates a number of variables that are crucial in determining how the trust evaluation unfolds. We will consider these variables as the **elements of trust context** that must be defined to indicate clearly what the context is.

So far, we have discussed a number of contextual differences in trust evaluation. First of all, the trust evaluation may refer to either a human or a computational agent trusting another entity (**cognitive trust vs. algorithmic trust**). In this brief, we use the term **cognition** to refer to human cognition only, in other words cases in which the trustor is a human. Clearly, for cognitive trust, one has to consider the impact of cognitive and social processing on trust evaluation. In the case of algorithmic trust, the trustor is a program and the algorithmic properties of the agent are a concern. Ultimately, cognitive trust uses a different system than algorithmic trust. While some algorithms are designed to mimic cognitive trust, others are not. Furthermore, the trustor is part of a network that provides her with different institutions that help or limit her actions in various ways.

Another important element of the trust context is the **trustor's goals** and the **trustee(s) she depends on** for these goals. The difference in the goals is apparent when the trust is for an action vs. when it is for information. For example, trusting Bob to perform a task is different than trusting the information given by Bob (**trust for actions vs. trust for information**). When discussing information trust, we note that it is different than information credibility. In fact, information credibility is a factor that may change the processing of information trust: credible information may not be trusted and trusted information may not be credible. For example, a highly trusted source may tell us that the building is on fire. The information is not credible, but the source is trustworthy. When evaluating the information trust, the trustor typically considers two things: the trust for the source of information and her own evaluation of the credibility of the message. Both of these are part of her goal. The trust evaluation may also take into account the network context. For example, the social network can be trusted to punish bad behavior and make it more likely that Bob will perform a specific action. In this example, both Bob and the network are trusted to some degree as part of the overall goal of the trustor. In short, trust evaluations involve complex goals with possibly multiple trustees.

Different trust goals lead to different concerns and processing. While many factors can be considered in evaluating trust goals, we will concentrate on two main classes: the **competence** and the **trustworthiness** of the trustee. Most trust goals can be mapped to either one or both of these classes of goals, which we will refer to as **trust constructs**. When relying on Bob to hold a secret, his trustworthiness is the most important concern. When relying on Bob to hold a heavy object, his physical capability is more relevant. Informativeness of signals varies depending on which trust construct is being considered. For example, trustworthiness is impacted by first impressions, especially by those obtained from facial attributes. For competence, first impressions may come from information related to the education and the training of an individual. Information obtained from the network and the trustor's firsthand experience with the trustee play a role for both constructs, but the trustor may pay more attention to positive evidence for competence and negative evidence for trustworthiness. Furthermore, one expects that competence is specific to a topic, while trustworthiness is a more general belief that applies to a large number of goals. In short, the goals and the underlying trust constructs determine which signals are important for trust evaluation and how evidence is evaluated.

The trust evaluation differs for different types of trustees in various ways; judging the trustworthiness of a person versus the trustworthiness of a robot may be quite different in terms of human cognition. As a result, the trustee may have an impact on how trust is evaluated.

Finally, external conditions such as the ordering of events and availability of different signals may also change the result of trust evaluation for the same trustee(s) and the same goal(s). This is especially true for human trustors. These dynamic considerations are part of the **trust evaluation environment**, which describes the conditions that impact the trust evaluation beyond the trustor, the trustee and the trustor's goals. They can be considered as a part of the dynamic properties of trust context. Note that these elements of context are not orthogonal categories; they are inter-related in many ways.

In summary, the trust context is a system level description of trust evaluation that takes as input the following variables/tunable parameters: (a) the trustor and the network she is operating in, (b) her goal(s) in making a trust evaluation and the underlying trust constructs, (c) the trustee(s) that she depends on, and (d) the environmental conditions that impact the trust evaluation. Next, we investigate the impact of each variable in trust evaluation in detail. However, we first describe the preconditions of trust that are common to all trust contexts.

Fig. 2.4 Trustor and trustee
in trust relationships

2.3.1 Preconditions of Trust

While the contexts we consider here are quite disparate, there are a number of
preconditions of trust that uniformly apply across all the different contexts we
consider. It is generally agreed that trust is a relationship involving two entities,
a trustor and a trustee. The strength of the relationship is used as a measure of trust.
The trustor trusts the trustee to accomplish a specific goal in a specific context.
Trust allows the trustor to take actions and make decisions under conditions of
uncertainty and from a position of **vulnerability** (Fig. 2.4) by **depending on the
trustee**. In a trust relationship, the trustor encounters uncertainty at the decision time
due to a lack of information or an inability to verify the integrity, the competence, the
positive intentions, and other characteristics of the trustee. The trustor is vulnerable
to suffering a loss if expectations of future outcomes turn out to be incorrect, i.e., if
her trust is misplaced. Vulnerability and uncertainty together can be summed up as
risk, the possibility that an action may lead to a loss.

2.3.1.1   Choices and Dependence

When making a trust evaluation, **dependence** describes to which degree the trustor
relies on the trustee for her specific goals (Fig. 2.5). Many outside factors may
determine the dependence. When judging trust for information, the ability of the
trustor to determine the credibility of the information is crucial. If the trustor is not
familiar with a specific topic, she may rely solely on the trustee's trustworthiness
and competence in determining information trust. When dealing with an unknown
trustee, the trustor may rely on the trustworthiness of a recommendation for that
trustee. The trustor depends on the trustee for a specific choice, sometimes called
as the **trusting choice**. For the decision to involve trust, there must be at least one
other choice in which the trustor does not depend on the trustee.

Fig. 2.5 The dependence on the trustee

Some definitions of trust also emphasize that the trustor should be able to reject a choice. Even if there is more than one choice to be made, it is possible that some of these choices are not desirable at all. According to our formulation, as long as there is one other choice in which the trustor does not depend on the trustee, then the dependence on the trustee involves trust. One can argue that for any action, there is always another choice, i.e., not to take that action. Some would argue the opposite, that our decisions are predetermined by our mental predispositions, especially in cases where we have not considered the pros and cons of different choices consciously. Without going into a deep discussion about free will, we would like to instead emphasize that dependence relations can vary greatly depending on the perception of the trustor as to what her choices are.

As an example, suppose Alan is painting the house with the help from his robot helper, Chip. Alan trusts Chip to hold the ladder steady so that he can paint high up. Thus, the trustor is Alan and the trustee is Chip. By trusting Chip, Alan is able to complete the task. If Alan did not trust Chip, he cannot use the ladder and cannot accomplish his task. Alan might consider other ways to paint these hard-to-reach locations, but he is convinced that they will produce lower-quality worksmanship.

2.3.1.2 Risk

Emphasized in the trust definition is the possibility to suffer negative consequences or to be disappointed if trust is misplaced. In other words, the trustor is made vulnerable as a result of trusting. The evaluation of consequences is generally encapsulated by a utility function, the perceived desirability of a situation according to the trustor. A positive consequence is considered to have positive utility. Similarly, negative consequences are determined by their negative utility. The desirability of different situations is subjective and may change from trustor to trustor. Various methods to formalize these preconditions of trust have been introduced. We summarize these conditions following conventions chosen by Wagner et al. [19]:

1. The trustor has more than one option to choose from. The trust decision is made before the trustee acts.
2. The outcome in the trusting option t depends on the trustee x. In the non-trusting option nt, the outcome does not depend on the trustee.
3. The trustor is better off if she chooses t instead of nt and the trustee ends up being trustworthy, given by a utility function U.
4. The trustor is worse off if she chooses t instead of nt and the trustee ends up being not trustworthy.

The first condition corresponds to our definition of options. The second condition describes the notion of dependence. The final two conditions describe the notion of risk.

In our example, if Chip fails in his duty, Alan will fall and badly injure himself. This situation clearly has low or negative utility. If Chip does as he is expected, Alan will finish his job successfully, a desirable condition with positive utility. If Alan does not trust Chip, other options will not produce a nice coat of paint and lead to lower utility than trusting Chip.

We sum up the above options by the equation of expected utility U:

$$U(trust \land x = bad) < U(not\ trust) < U(trust \land x = good)$$

It has long been argued whether the above elements can describe what trust is. The above are conditions that exist in all situations requiring trust: the presence of choices, the dependence on the trustee in the trusting choice, the uncertainty and the vulnerability of the trustor at the decision time. However, these conditions are not necessarily complete since they abstract out elements like the common understanding of expectations between the trustor and the trustee. Many sophisticated computational trust models have been developed with the aim of understanding how people trust others or for building agents that can trust another entity.

Trust is affected by the trustor's knowledge of her environment, as perceived by her. The environment provides her with input relevant to trust where the relevance is determined by her goals. Exactly how the environment and the trustor's knowledge impacts trust is typically part of the trust model implicitly. However, we will make this aspect of trust models explicit by our emphasis on the trust context in a wide range of applications. We will not concentrate on a single formalism for modeling trust, but instead we will describe how contextual elements change the trust models.

Next, we describe the crucial elements of trust context.

2.3.2 Decision Maker: The Trustor

Trust is studied in social sciences as a human construct. When people make decisions, trust allows them to choose one decision over the others by relying on each other. The trustee can be another person, a team or an organization. However, only a human being can trust a trustee. Even when discussing organizations trusting other organizations, social sciences take the view that decisions in organizations are made by human decision makers. In essence, the trust literature in this area aims to analyze how and why people trust others, how trust impacts their behavior and how systems can be devised to achieve certain social outcomes by influencing trust. Various perspectives shed light on this relationship: their social network, cognitive heuristics and biases and specific goals. Some researchers, for example concentrate on how people form opinions of others. There is also research in how different traits of a person affect their trust relationships or how emotions impact trust. Other researchers may look at various social advantages offered by trusting relationships. Some studies concentrate on how people attribute positive and negative features to different social groups that impact their trust. In some approaches, people are modeled as agents acting in self-interest and trying to modify their own utility. In this case, trust is a way of achieving future gains and systems designed to calibrate people's utilities can impact their trust.

These different approaches sometimes conflict with each other. There is continuing debate on whether human beings are rational [9]. If rationality is described as adherence to the assumptions of mathematical utility theory, there are many findings about how people make decisions that are at odds with this notion of rationality. Ultimately, human decision making depends on the trustor's view of the world; her value system, what she knows and remembers, and the cognitive process she uses to make a decision all play a role. However, these conditions are not fully known externally. All trust models with a human trustor operates with an underlying set of assumptions about how people evaluate trust. Sometimes these assumptions are explicit, and sometimes they are embedded in complex algorithms. Regardless of how these assumptions are defined, they are an approximation of human decision making.

In our previous examples, Chip trusted Alan also. Is this a new type of trust? Chip is evaluating trust using an algorithm based on a model of trust. In computing, a large number of trust models are proposed. Some attempt to mimic the cognitive trust by incorporating how trust beliefs form and are used in decision making [1, 10]. Some models do not have a social cognitive component, but attempt to assess properties of trustworthy entities and introduce optimal protocols for trusting. For example, an algorithm for routing in mobile ad-hoc networks measures how well each node is behaving to assess whether they are working properly and are not compromised [6]. The algorithm then concludes that a computational node can trust another. Another notion of trust is introduced by ranking algorithms, which try to assess which sites are likely to have more reliable links and updates its rank computation by valuing the links from these sites more highly [7]. These models of trust are often based on observations of network behavior that incorporate system based and human input. For example, web sites are created and maintained by people aided by applications that automate many tasks. Trust for both needs to be taken into account. The algorithmic models of trust may differ from cognitive aspects of trust in many different ways. For example, they may incorporate fine-tuned processing of the environment with attention to statistical properties of different variables, criteria rarely considered in cognitive processing. They may also make some simplifying assumptions, disregarding inputs crucial to cognitive models.

In short, the trustor describes the underlying trust model. The trust model describes the trust evaluation system and how trust evaluation changes depending on context. We still distinguish between two broad classes of trust models. The first class, called cognitive trust tries to closely resemble cognitive and social processing of trust signals. The second class, called computational trust, is not strictly based how people trust each other, even though it may borrow some terminology from cognitive trust. A trust model may fall anywhere between these two broad classes.

It is debatable when a trust model can be called purely computational, not based on any cognitive model. This is a topic of study in many agent-based trust models where different cognitive components are introduced into trust models. An example of such a model is one in which agents evaluate trustees' actions based on their current trust beliefs of their trustworthiness. For our purposes, it is not important to draw this line accurately. What is important is to appreciate that many different system level descriptions of trust exist depending on who the trustor is.

2.3.3 The Trustor's Goals and Trust Constructs

In the previous sections, we gave many examples of cases in which the trustor had a choice in which she depends on a trustee to accomplish a certain goal. We have also shown cases in which the trustor's goal is complex and depends on multiple trustees. In this section, we will further discuss how the trust goal can be complex along two dimensions: the subgoals that make up a goal and the constructs used to evaluate trust for each construct. In particular, we make a distinction between information trust and action trust. We first start by discussing these two.

2.3.3.1 Evaluating Information Trust

We have seen that the trustor considers two separate subgoals when deciding whether or not to trust certain information.

- First, does she trust the information source to provide information that can be trusted?
- Second, does she trust herself to evaluate the credibility of the information?

The trustor is dependent both on herself and the source of information for this trust evaluation. How much weight each subgoal carries in the final evaluation of trust depends on many factors, one of which is the familiarity of the trustor with the information topic. If the trustor knows very little about a specific topic, her trust for the information may rely almost completely on her trust in the information source.

The information trust evaluation may involve other subgoals. Similar to the telephone game, online information travels through many media and can be altered along the way by people as well as programs. The trustor is also dependent on the entities that were involved in the transmission of a message. She may consider how much she trusts the transmission media as part of her information trust evaluation.

Suppose Alice sees facebook a post by Bob that says: "I lost 10 lbs on this amazing new diet, take a look at the following web site!" Alice may find it quite unlikely that Bob would post this type of information, and considers the possibility that this is spam. In this case, she does not trust this information. However, this is not due to her trust for Bob. She doubts the credibility of the message and considers the possibility that Bob's account used in this post was compromised. As a result, she attributes the message to someone other than Bob. This subgoal is sometimes referred to as the identity trust, which is the trust that the poster is in fact who he says he is. Note that identity trust is not necessarily an independent trust goal; it is likely evaluated conditionally.

In another example, suppose Alice is watching a video in which Bob is supporting a certain point of view. Again, Alice finds it unlikely that this video reflects Bob's true opinion. She may then consider the possibility that video may have been edited to alter its meaning. This may be due to the fact that the trust for the source presenting the video is not trustworthy. In these examples, the entities involved in the transmission and editing of information are conditionally considered in the trust assessment and are subgoals of information trust.

As a different example, suppose Alice and Bob are walking to a restaurant. Bob tells Alice that the restaurant is at 45th St, so Alice trusts him. It is possible that Bob got his information from Google Maps, but he has not told this to Alice. If he did, then Alice would base her trust evaluation on Google Maps' reliability, not Bob's. The trustee is in fact determined by the perceived source of the information. Alice could have also considered Bob's ability to look up Google Maps, but probably that would be a bit insulting. Here, Bob could be considered the transmission medium for this information.

Let us now consider a crowdsourcing system that uses a large amount of input, from many sources. The main assumption behind such a system is that if sufficient number of independent sources of information are consulted, then the final answer will be trustworthy regardless of how trustworthy each individual is. The design of this system in fact significantly reduces the dependence on any individual information source. The trust for information in such a system depends predominantly on the design of the system: how it collects and aggregates information. The properties of the underlying population of information providers are also a crucial part of assessing trust. Such a system provides an institution that supports trust, and depends on the trustworthiness of its inputs. We will examine many examples of these types of institutions in the next chapters.

In short, trust for information may depend on a number of subgoals such as how much the perceived source of information is trusted to provide trustworthy information, how much the various entities along the information transmission path can be trusted to deliver it correctly, and how credible the information appears to the trustor.

2.3.3.2 Evaluating Trust for Actions

When trusting another entity to accomplish a specific task, the trustor's goal is determined by the given task. Suppose Alice is buying a book from an online seller, Bob. She pays Bob for the book. At this point, Alice is fully depending on Bob to send the book, and Bob controls the outcome of this transaction completely. Alice's goal is to get the book from Bob. What guarantees that Bob will not take the money and run? This is a topic of very old debate. Is it the fear of sanctions from the community? Is it the promise of future rewards for Bob if he cooperates? Is it morality and expected behavior patterns? Are these fundamentally different things?

Regardless of the underlying assumptions of why people honor contracts, we note that there are many institutions that constrain Bob's actions. These could be social institutions based on expected behavior, or institutions providing legal protections. Many online services provide computational reputation mechanisms that serve as a soft form of legal protection. Bob's reputation as a seller allows him to continue selling to other customers. The reputation management mechanism guarantees that if he misbehaves, this reputation will be damaged. As a result, he has reason to act trustworthy. In this instance, Alice is dependent on the effectiveness of the reputation system for her purchase in addition to her dependence on Bob.

Reputation management is also referred to as trust management in some computing literature. Some argue that this is not an appropriate term. In fact, trust management schemes of this form reduce the need for trust instead of enhancing it [4]. Instead, we define this as a shift of dependence from one trustee (Bob) to another (the reputation system), either partially or completely. A reputation system cannot completely eliminate Alice's dependence on Bob for arbitrary online markets, especially if Bob can easily create another online identity as soon as his current reputation is ruined. To this day, identity management is one of the most important problems in online transactions [2, 15]. To address this, the reputation system may require a history of transactions. Such a requirement may end up increasing the cost of entry into the market, which may not be desirable.

Alice's goals may be more complex than the successful completion of a task. She also cares about the likelihood that the product will be shipped quickly, will be packed well, and will arrive undamaged. Reputation alone may not be sufficient to support all these goals and additional institutional mechanisms may be needed, each resulting in a different dependency.

Similar considerations exist when the trustee is a computational agent or a robot. Alice needs to trust the robot, the specific piece of hardware that she is interacting with, to be in good operating condition. Furthermore, she needs to trust the underlying programming of the robot to be capable and trustworthy.

In short, similar to the case of information trust, for a specific trusting choice, there might be multiple goals and trustees. In such a case, the trustor depends on each trustee to some degree. Each trustee has some level of control over the outcome of the goal through a specific subgoal.

2.3.3.3 Trust Constructs: Trustworthiness and Competence

As we have seen in the discussion of information and action based trust, the trustor typically has a complex goal involving subgoals. Each subgoal defines the evaluation of specific aspects of the trustee. Trust research has generated a long list of keywords used in this effort, such as goodness, morality, benevolence, expertness, credibility, predictability, dependability, etc. There have been many efforts to categorize these considerations into distinct types [11,17]. We will review these in the next chapter.

In the case of trusting actions, an often-used categorization separates trustworthiness from ability.

Trustworthiness refers to our expectation that a person will do as they say. This term incorporates dimensions like the trustee's integrity and good intentions.

Ability is the trustee's competence in accomplishing a specific task (Fig. 2.6).

A trustworthy person may be dependable for completing a task, but their performance may not be satisfactory if they are not capable.

In reputation management, a system designed to force people to act in a trustworthy manner may sanction bad behavior [2]. However, sanctioning alone is not sufficient to separate competent but untrustworthy people from incompetent but trustworthy people. To assess the ability of people, online reviews have been found to be more useful [3]. These are called signaling mechanisms. For trustworthiness, tracking bad behavior is considered more diagnostic, while for ability, tracking and accumulation of good behavior is more meaningful. This agrees with research that explains how people form opinions of others [5]. Trustworthiness is a general measure of the trustee's reliability and is not dependent on a specific topic. If someone is our friend, we expect that he will do what he says and will help us when we ask for it. However, ability is dependent on a topic: a doctor's competence is in medicine and a mechanic's is in car repair.

Some research also concentrates on a third type of trust construct. In this case, the intentions of the trustees are considered [14]. Even if Bob does not act in a way that Alice prefers, he may still have Alice's best interests at heart. Sometimes these are called **good intentions**. An adversary with bad intentions may act in a trustworthy way to achieve advantages that he may later use against the trustor. In cognitive psychology, the evaluations of another's intent are studied as part of the theory of mind. According to this theory, people learn about other's beliefs and

Fig. 2.6 Competence of the trustee

thoughts by comparing them to themselves [12, 13]. Our understanding of ourselves and others evolves over time through shared social activities and cultural learning. These activities create a common set of expected behavioral patterns and social norms [18]. In short, we tend to think that people who act and talk like us probably think like us and have similar intentions. We project ourselves onto others. In-group and out-group dynamics and friend or foe categories typically result in judgments of intent. Those who are in the in-group are associated with positive intent, while those in the out-group are perceived as having negative intent. Due to the close links of good intentions to the trustworthiness dimension, most categorizations consider only the first two constructs for trust. However, most point out that an untrustworthy person is treated very differently than a person with bad intent, i.e., a distrusted person for whom trustworthiness is considered negative. When an untrusworthy person starts to act trustworthy, trust may eventually develop. However, a distrusted person's trustworthy actions may be met with suspicision and disregarded. As a result, trust may never develop. A simple example of this type distrust can be seen between individuals from social groups that have historically been in conflict. The burden of proof is much higher in these cases for trust relationships to develop.

Research in information trust [8] shows that people use various different constructs in this case as well such as truthfulness, believability, accuracy, objectivity, timeliness or reliability. It is also possible to classify these into two main categories. Truthfulness is more of an affective factor that represents a dependence on the trustworthiness of the source. Accuracy and timeliness on the other hand, are more closely linked to the competence of the source. Similar to ability, they are specific to a topic. In essence, parallel notions of trustworthiness and competence of the sources exist when considering information.

Believability, on the other hand, can be tied more closely to the information itself and the trustor's evaluation of it. As we discussed earlier, evaluation of information trust also involves the trustor's evaluations of the information. As this subgoal involves only the trustor, we can also consider this as a significant component of the trust evaluation context.

Trust goals generally map to constructs that fall in these very general classes, but they can be much more specific. Alan trusts his doctor to diagnose him correctly (competence) and tell him the truth (trustworthiness). He trusts Chip to hold the ladder so he does not fall (competence). Alice trusts Google Maps to have the correct answer (competence) and have the best coverage of location information (competence). Alice trusts Wikipedia to have the most objective (trustworthiness of the source) and the most comprehensive (competence of the source) information on a topic. Alice trusts Bob to send her purchase quickly as he promises (trustworthiness), and the electronic marketplace to provide accurate information about Bob (trustworthiness) and reduce his reputation score if she gives a bad comment (trustworthiness).

All these subgoals describe a trust construct and a trustee that the trustor is dependent on for that construct. Is there a distinction between how competence and trustworthiness are evaluated when the trustee is a person vs. when it is an automated system? This is a topic of research. We will review some of the literature on this issue in the next chapter.

2.3.4 Trust Evaluation: Cues, Network and Time Effects

The final critical component of trust context is the environment in which trust is evaluated. There are some significant effects that must be considered when human cognition is involved. We review some of these issues in this section. One can also find parallel issues of concern in the design of algorithms that compute trust. We will review those in Chap. 4.

The first effect we have discussed at length is the credibility of the information that is being considered. We have seen the complex decision making process involved in deciding whether to trust information or not. The source's trustworthiness may trump the credibility of information in some cases, and in other cases the reverse may happen.

Let's go back to Alice and Bob walking to the restaurant that Bob thinks is at 45th St. Even though Alice remembers quite well that it is around 34th, she decides to believe Bob. After a long walk, they reach 45th Street and find out that the restaurant is not there. A quick search reveals that in fact Bob's online source was wrong; Alice was right all along. She knew this, too! Why did she believe Bob? A well-known fact is that we are willing to override our own evaluations of information, even when we are quite sure, by those of a so-called expert. Often we say that we knew it all along, but still somehow ended up believing someone else. The reason is that evaluating information and reconciling conflicts take cognitive effort. Often, we are not willing to spend this effort unless we do not trust the source completely or some other outside conditions prime us to do so. Hence, the dependence for the information could change drastically depending on the situation.

Utilities are discussed in almost all trust research to define what the trustor expects to gain or lose in various situations. For cognitive trust, how the choices are framed makes a big difference. For example, people value gains and losses differently. Framing the same situation as a potential gain or a potential loss that is averted may impact the decision greatly. The other well-known factor is the endowment effect: we will value something that we own much more than an equivalent item that is not ours. When multiple options are presented, the desirability of an option may also change when an irrelevant option is added. All of this points to the inevitable conclusion that utility is not a simple value evaluation: the framing effects must be considered in trust evaluation [9].

Almost all trust computation is based on a set of cues that are used to assess the trust for the trustees with respect to the specific goals. People use these cues daily, and computational models aim to mimic the human cognitive process. The social cognition of others is based on many different cues, including their faces, their social position, the stories we hear about them (social reputation) and our own experience with them. A similar set of cues exists for text, ranging from the appearance of the content to the authority of the source. We also form opinions of other entities, such as computer systems, information systems, or intelligent agents helping us using many similar cues. We will examine these in detail in the next chapter. We note that at the cognitive level, some of these cues are very easy to execute while others require effort. Kahneman [9] argues that cues that are less costly to process are more frequently used than those that are more costly. Furthermore, the order in which we evaluate cues may impact the trust evaluation; for example, when interacting with a person with an untrustworthy face, it may take us longer to trust them since trustworthiness of faces is processed much more quickly, and the resulting first impressions may impact our subsequent evaluations of trust.

Where the trustor's past experience of the trustee is concerned, some models consider all past experience, while some models consider that the trustor can forget or forgive various past events. The other important factor to consider is priming. For example, people who have been reading about social justice may view an article about wealth distribution differently than those who have been reading about problems with the welfare system. Priming is a well-known effect and used frequently by those involved in advertising or political propaganda. Different external cues may alter the evaluation of information credibility for the same article.

The other thing to remember is that the processing capability of the trustor plays a role in how much of the relevant input will be considered when making a decision. When we are busy or tired, we have fewer cognitive resources and may rely on simpler cues to evaluate trust. For example, relying on Bob's information about the restaurant's location was quite simple. It did not require Alice to think at all about whether the location is indeed incorrect by retrieving information about past visits from her own memory. It was much easier to acquiesce to Bob's opinion, especially at the end of the day when Alice was tired and hungry.

When considering networking effects, the nature of social relations can also be relevant. For example, an often debated issue is whether or not trust is transitive or not. Ultimately, it depends on the underlying social and trust context. For example, transitive closure is often found in social relations involving close friends. This is because two of Alice's friends end up hanging out together and become friends.

Friendship in this sense is a symmetric relation, and transitive closure implies that trust between friends is transitive. This is also reflected in the way we evaluate the intentions of others. Our friends have positive intentions towards us. However, not all friends are considered competent for a specific goal. There is no reason to expect that ability is symmetric or transitive. We will investigate this issue in more detail in the later chapters. Clearly, transitivity is an assumption that may apply to some trust constructs but not all.

Similar considerations exist when computational trust is concerned. The cues used to assess trust must be useful, and free of bias as much as possible. System design must take into account how to correctly optimize for trust. For example, a crowdsourcing system that makes previous votes available to voters introduces a bias towards the votes of the earlier voters. There is reason not to trust such a system. In our opinion, these issues impact trust computation greatly but have not yet been discussed in great detail.

In summary, we must consider which cues are available to the trustor to judge trust as well as the trustor's goals. Factors in the environment may impact how the trustor's choices are framed and whether the trustor is primed to evalute them in a specific way. The mental load and alertness of the trustor may impact which factors will be evaluated. The order in which factors become available and are evaluated may change the final trust evaluation. The relevant enviromental factors depend on the trust constructs and trustees. Modeling these factors is an important part of any trust model.

2.3.5 tl;dr

A common norm in online sites is to complete a long chunk of text with a section called tl;dr (Too Long Didn't Read). This section summarizes the trust context in a few sentences to accommodate readers with limited cognitive resources.

The trust context defines who the trustor is and who the trustees are. The dependence for a specific trusting choice specifies in detail which trustee to depend on for which goal and how much. A utility is defined for each specific choice, which in turn is used in defining trust.

However, to evaluate trust, a set of external cues regarding the trustees must be used based on the environmental factors. Their evaluation is greatly impacted by a set of external factors that need to be considered when modeling and measuring trust.

References

1. C. Castelfranchi, R. Falcone, *Trust Theory: A Socio-Cognitive and Computational Model* (Wiley, 2010)
2. C. Dellarocas, Reputation mechanism design in online trading environments with pure moral hazard. Inf. Syst. Res. **16**(2), 209–230 (2005)

3. C. Dellarocas, X.M. Zhang, N.F. Awad, Exploring the value of online product reviews in forecasting sales: The case of motion pictures. J. Interact. Mark. **21**(4), 23–45 (2007)

4. D. Elgesem, Normative structures in trust management, in *Proceedings of the 4th International Conference on Trust Management*, Pittsburgh, PA, pp. 48–61 (2006)

5. S.T. Fiske, A.J. Cuddy, P. Glick, Universal dimensions of social cognition: warmth and competence. Trends. Cognit. Sci. **11**(2), 77–83 (2007)

6. K. Govindan, P. Mohapatra, Trust computations and trust dynamics in mobile adhoc networks: a survey. IEEE Commun. Surv. Tutor. **14**(2), 279–298 (2011)

7. Z. Gyongyi, H. Garcia-Molina, J. Pedersen, Combating web spam with trustrank, in *Proceedings of the 30th International Conference on Very Large Data Bases*, Toronto, 2004

8. B. Hilligoss, S.Y. Rieh, Developing a unifying framework of credibility assessment: construct, heuristics and interaction in context. Inf. Process. Manag. **44**, 1467–1484 (2008)

9. D. Kahneman, *Thinking, Fast and Slow* (Farrar, Straus and Giroux, New York, 2011)

10. S.P. Marsh, *Formalising trust as a computational concept*. PhD thesis, University of Stirling, 1994

11. D.H. McKnight, N.L. Chervany, What trust means in e-commerce customer relationships: an interdisciplinary conceptual typology. Int. J. Electron. Commer. **6**, 35–59 (2001)

12. A.N. Meltzoff, 'Like me': a foundation for social cognition. Dev. Sci. **10**(1), 126–134 (2007)

13. A.N. Meltzoff, R. Brooks, Self-experience as a mechanism for learning about others: a training study in social cognition. Dev. Psychol. **44**(5), 1257–1265 (2008)

14. M.C. Moldoveanu, J.A.C. Baum, "I think you think i think you're lying": the interactive epistemology of trust in social networks. Manag. Sci. **57**(2), 393–412 (2011)

15. H. Nissenbaum, Will security enhance trust online, or supplant it? in *Trust and Distrust in Organizations* ed. by R.M. Kramer, K.S. Cook. Russell Sage Series on Trust (Russell Sage Foundation, New York, 2004) pp. 155–188

16. D.M. Rousseau, S.B. Sitkin, R.S. Burt, C. Camerer, Not so different after all: a cross-discipline view of trust. Acad. Manag. Rev. **23**, 393–404 (1998)

17. F.D. Schoorman, R.C. Mayer, J.H. Davis, An integrative model of organizational trust: past, present and future. Acad. Manag. Rev. **32**(2), 344–354 (2007)

18. M. Tomasello, M. Carpenter, J. Call, T. Behne, H. Moll, Understanding and sharing intentions: the origins of cultural cognition. Behav. Brain Sci. **28**(5),675–91; discussion 691–735 (2005)

19. A.R. Wagner, R.C. Arkin, Recognizing situations that demand trust, in *International Symposium on Robots and Human Interactive Communications*, IEEE RO-MAN, Atlanta, 2011

Chapter 3
Trust as a Social and Cognitive Construct

In this chapter, we concentrate on the study of trust as a social and cognitive construct. In particular, we concentrate on the role social networks and social institutions play in how people trust each other. A person's trust for a specific institution impacts their trust evaluations as the trustor is able to draw inferences based on the role the trustee plays in an institution. This is especially important when firsthand experience with the trustee is not possible. Even when the trustee is known to the trustor, the institutions may still be part of the trust context in different ways. We examine these in detail in this chapter.

We review social cognition research that concentrates on how people perceive others. In relationships with other people, two distinct attributes play a role in trust evaluation: the trustworthiness and the competence of the trustee. We show that these two attributes are also discussed in relation to different social institutions. This helps us frame the dependence component of trust in better detail. We also review work that discusses trust for automated systems and to which degree this construct is similar to and different from trust for another person. This helps us understand how the dependence relations may change when the trustee is not a person. Finally, we review some of the work on trusting information, in particular, networked information processing. These studies also outline the view of trust involving a complex goal and underline the importance of the trustor's confidence in the given topic area as well as the trust for the information source.

3.1 Trust and Institutions

Social institutions take many forms. Social networks and culture operate on an informal but commonly-agreed set of norms and behavior patterns. On the other hand, legal and economic institutions are based on formal sets of rules and protocols that describe what constitutes acceptable behavior. In general, these systems help promote actions that require trust, either between individuals or other actors in society. This is typically the result of the role the institution plays in reducing the risk involved in such interactions. The trustor's dependence on the trustee is reduced thanks to the institutional expectations that promote good behavior and enforcement mechanisms that penalize bad behavior [62]. To fully understand how institutions achieve this moderating function, we first examine a number of different institutions and their impact on trust.

3.1.1   Trust in a Social Context

Trust is a foundational aspect of social relations. It is often studied in the context of transactions, both economic and non-economic. Some characterizations view trust from a market perspective. Coleman introduces the notion of time as a crucial precondition of trust in transactions [8]. In a market where transactions occur over a period of time, one party delivers certain goods or makes an investment. The exchange in response to this investment will occur at a later time. As a result, the investor is hoping or expecting that the other parties involved in the transaction will complete the transaction as planned. This transactional aspect concentrates on the actions of others and how they control the resources. The risk inherent in these transactions comes from the possible loss of resources that are invested in the transaction or from the loss of opportunity. The dependence comes from the level of control the trustee has over the resources.

The notion of utility is generally used to capture the costs and the benefits of the transactions. Social theories differ in how utility is defined. Economic models consider a self-interested agent who wants to maximize her utility. Market mechanisms define the cost of transactions by incorporating the many different concerns of the parties involved in the transactions. The main question in such an approach is whether the market prices incorporate all possible risk in the interactions. If that is the case, the decision to trust is reduced to one of risk management. The trustor needs to choose the appropriate risk that she is willing to accept for a certain amount of expected utility. Such a system does not incorporate the trustor's long-term dependence on the trustee and assumes that the trustor depends on the trustee for a single transaction. However, if the trustee does not perform as expected, then the trustor is free to move to a different trustee at the appropriate market price and the trustee will face negative consequences imposed by the market.

In contrast with the economic view where individuals maximize utility, some social and cultural models aim to explain behavior as a function of the costs that society imposes on individuals through sanctions. In this model, individuals choose behavior patterns that are acceptable within the social groups to which they belong. The social norms and expectations define the costs associated with different courses of action. For example, fulfilling a contract is a socially accepted behavior and failing to do so will result in a sanction imposed by society. The trustors depend on the enforcement of the social norms, which is a form of public good. Either all will enforce these norms or they are not useful to anyone. One of the common criticisms of this model is that it does not explain the motives of the individuals properly. Individuals are not only avoiding sanctions, but also seeking to gain some utility. These efforts may sometimes be at odds with actions that create public goods. In other words, what are the goals of the individuals for conducting different transactions? If they are selfishly trying to maximize their utility, they might not be willing to incur a cost to sanction another to benefit the public good. Without the efforts of others, social norms will not be very effective.

3.1.1.1 Embeddedness

In the context of economic transactions, the social theory based on embeddedness [21] explains how these two theories can be combined. A central observation in this theory is that there are many cases in which market prices do not take into account all possible costs associated with transactions and institutional structures alone cannot guard against misbehavior. In this case, the economic view does not offer sufficient tools to suppress fraud and malfeasance. However, social mechanisms based on trust can help explain how individuals manage risk associated with such transactions. The trust in this case is dependent on the social context, i.e., the content, history and structural location of the ties between individuals. If people have interacted with each other in the past, this helps them form expectations about the future and assess risk more accurately. According to Granovetter [21], social norms or morality play a central role only when there is no social context. For example, when deciding to give a tip at a restaurant that will never be visited again, norms play a role. It is an expected behavior to tip someone, but the sanctions can only impact the individual at an emotional level if she misbehaves. In all other cases, the social network the individual is embedded in helps shape her behavior.

In support of this hypotheses, Granovetter lists a number of ways social ties and trust help reduce the different risks associated with transactions. The central objective of the trustor is to reduce the risk associated with a transaction due to possible deceit by the trustee. The trustee, on the other hand, wants to be trusted by others in future transactions. However, the underlying motivations for the trustee to act in a trustworthy manner go deeper than a desire to achieve a good global reputation, especially in a setting in which the same trustor and trustee are likely to interact again. If the only reason for acting trustworthy was to achieve good reputation, this would almost equate reputation to a network-wide commodity. However, both the trustor and the trustee are able to draw unique advantages from their pairwise trust relationship that goes far beyond achieving good reputation. Since the trustor has firsthand experience with the trustee and there is an expectation of future interactions, it is less likely that the trustee will misbehave. Furthermore, establishing continued relationships with the trustee reduces the risks and costs associated with searching for and establishing relationships with a new trustee. Another important concern is the ability to resolve problems with the trustee. Continued interactions allow the trustor and the trustee to learn the best methods for effective communication, hence reducing the cost of future communications. This is referred to as learning to work together. In fact, such continued relationships allow the exchange of privileged information between the trustor and the trustee about important topics. For example, in transactions between organizations, accurate information about employees can be very valuable when making new hiring decisions.

However, Granovetter also points out that trust can also lead to vulnerabilities in which a trusted party can more easily misbehave and cause more harm. In addition, social structures can help foster untrustworthy behavior by supporting coalitions between actors involved in fraud. Such structures may allow larger-scale fraudulent activities by allowing different parties to better organize their actions.

In short, trust evaluations incorporate multiple considerations, i.e., complex goals and dependencies. An efficient market structure does not obviate the need for existing social relationships that an individual may draw resources from. On the other extreme, positive firsthand experience with a trustee is not necessarily sufficient to trust someone. The trustor is still dependent on the social network for continued trustworthy behavior from the trustee.

3.1.1.2 Social Capital

The benefits conferred by a specific social context are summarized by the term "social capital" [7]. The term is meant to show that the social network can serve as a shared social good. Similar to the terms financial and human capital, social capital allows individuals to take actions that may not be possible or are too costly without it. The social capital lies not in the specific individuals but in the totality of the relationships. For example, the safety of individuals is not only protected by the police but also by social norms that are maintained by the vigilance of a social group. This social capital benefits all the members of the group, for example by allowing them to walk freely at night without fear of danger. Similarly, while a university provides valuable education to individuals, it also provides them with close relationships that they can later rely on to get privileged information in their business.

One of Coleman's examples describes the close and dense relationships in the wholesale diamond market. This network enables the participants to trust a valuable commodity like diamonds to a member of the group without any explicit insurance, enabling fast and efficient transactions. The fact that participants in this network all know each other well makes such an action possible. If one of the members misbehaves, he will be sanctioned by all the members of the group and suffer great losses. In fact, closure, i.e., the degree to which the friends of a friend know each other, is one of the main social structures that makes the creation of social capital possible. Closure is especially crucial to the social capital of trustworthiness, since it provides a social mechanism for enforcing obligations. Organizations that have been formed for a specific purpose can also serve as the basis of a social network of ties that can be mobilized to create social capital in new contexts. In fact, if individuals are linked in more than one context (e.g. both neighbor and fellow worker), they can bring to bear the resources available in one context to the other. One can consider social capital to be a public good, where the creators do not necessarily benefit themselves and do not necessarily act with the intention of creating social capital. However, its availability provides the members with unique benefits.

Social capital forms a type of institution that the individuals may depend on. In this context, the social structure creates an environment where obligations and expectations of certain type of behavior are likely to be honored by its members. Hence, in the transactional sense of trust, the trustor depends on the social structure to reduce the risk associated with new transactions, and to provide timely and privileged information to the participants.

3.1.1.3 Embedded Versus Arm's Length Ties

Uzzi [72] elaborates on this concept further by studying organizations in New York's apparel industry. In this industry, the cost of entry is low which would favor a competitive market. However, Uzzi finds a great deal of embedded links in this industry in which participants work with each other repeatedly, providing special pricing or favors to each other over time. Uzzi discusses the benefits of such links, such as access to quick and fine-grained information, joint problem-solving ability and overall trust in transactions. He reports that most embedded relationships start with the help of third-party referral networks and over time become embedded.

In contrast with the previous work, Uzzi also points out that despite the many benefits of embedded links, when organizations rely on these links too heavily, other risks arise. For example, in very tight networks, organizations may end up making non-optimal business decisions to maintain these embedded links and fulfill obligations. Furthermore, this also limits the ability of the organization to obtain novel ideas, access unique products, and hence improve its competitiveness. In fact, through quantitative analysis, he shows that the most successful firms use a combination of embedded links and arm's length links. While interactions on embedded links rely on a heuristic decision making process, the interactions along the arm's length links use calculative and market-based decision making strategies. The benefits of these dual types of links have been shown for different industries; for example in Broadway musicals, teams with a mix of long lasting relationships as well as "fresh blood" tend to be the most successful ones [73]. Teams that rely solely on embedded links lose opportunities for innovations. Listening to only one's friends can create an echo chamber where everyone knows the same information and has the same opinion. Teams with many changes in their membership have higher costs of maintenance and do not benefit sufficiently from closer relationships. The optimal approach for teams is to maintain embedded links for stability, but also pay the additional cost to incorporate some new members periodically to broaden the talent pool of the team.

One of the important implications of the social aspect of trust, as explained by the embeddedness of individuals in a social network is that social mechanisms are likely to play a major role in the formation and maintenance of trust relationships.

For example, triadic closure means that two people with a common friend are likely to be connected to each other as well [14]. One expects that triadic closure is much more likely to apply to trust relations exhibiting embeddedness. However, not all possible trust relations will exhibit this property, especially those formed by arm's length relationships. In essence, trust relations in the context of embeddedness relate closely to the "trustworthiness" dimension of relationships, while arm's length relationships are based on specific external criteria and hence are closer to the "competence" dimension.

A later study by Kollock and Braziel [33] points to importance of the social relationships in an online setting. The authors examine the failure of many B2B (business to business) ventures. They point out that these efforts were partially based on the assumption that a market involving anonymous buyers and sellers will be more successful than one that relies on social relationships. However, the failure of these approaches shown that assumption does not hold in real life. One the reasons is offered by McFadden: "Real-life markets are very rough, murky, tumultuous places where commodity attributes shift, supply is uncertain, prices volatile, and information imperfect" [43]. This further resonates with the observation that markets do not incorporate all possible risk into prices. In these cases, trust based on past interactions reduces the risk associated with a transaction. When future interactions are unlikely to occur, then additional mechanisms are needed to enhance the market prices. Examples of these are reputation methods that we will examine in later sections.

To summarize, the social network that an individual is embedded in provides her with special privileges both in economic and non-economic contexts. The trustor can rely on a trustee for a number of different goals: achieving a task in a timely and cost-effective manner, resolving conflicts easily, and obtaining information that will offer a competitive advantage. The social structure provides the necessary enforcement mechanisms that limit the trustee's ability to misbehave. These in turn reduce the inherent risk and uncertainty involved in the transaction. Therefore, the trustor depends on the social network for her actions. However, even in the case of repeated transactions, relying solely on trusted entities is not always optimal. Trustees outside the trustor's social network may have access to information or resources of strategic value. Even though interactions with such trustees may involve higher levels of uncertainty and risk, the may be worth the cost. Hence, when evaluating trust in a transactional context, there are a multitude of different goals that can be important to the trust decision. These goals are all part of the trust context and exactly describe the dependence of the trustor on the trustee.

3.1.2 Trust in Economic Institutions

In the previous section, we considered trust relations within a social context where the concepts of embeddedness and social capital play a large role. These trust relations can be of an economic nature, business relationships between firms, or

Fig. 3.1 Trust in economic institutions

they can be based on social interactions, such as parents of children or neighbors participating in activities that benefit others. For example, embedded social relationships and the social capital that they provide enable parents to trust other parents to monitor their children, or neighbors to trust others to watch out for their property. However, there are many other institutions that are relied on for different actions. Formal law, organizational rules, and norms impose sanctions on those who break the rules through various enforcement mechanisms. These institutions are crucial when interacting with a trustee who is not part of one's social network. They allow the trustor to assess a baseline for the amount of risk she is exposing herself to in a specific interaction. In this section, we will discuss some of these institutions (Fig. 3.1).

Carruthers [4] discusses the role various institutions play in determining how much one person trusts another in credit transactions. In these transactions, the seller extends credit to a buyer who receives goods and in return provides a promise to pay at a future date. The seller has to trust that the buyer is going to fulfill her promise, the receipt of the payment. However, there is uncertainty about whether the trustee will in fact honor the debt. As a result, the trustor is vulnerable to losing money if the trust is misplaced. Carruthers illustrates the function of various financial institutions by discussing the historical development of credit in the U.S. in which different institutions emerged to reduce the uncertainty and vulnerability faced by lenders and to enhance their willingness to trust the debtors.

Some of these institutions are informational: they provide information about the debtor that is not easy to obtain without social relationships, and may even be hard to get through social channels. For example, the character and reputation of the debtor and the purpose for the loan are the types of information that one tends to obtain through social channels. These channels may lead to biased evaluations of the trustees due to the lack of ability to compare with others or reliance on subjective measures. To address this problem, many specialized institutions have emerged over time to provide information about the past transactions and the financial health of the debtor. Examples of such institutions are the Mercantile Agency in the 1880s, Standard and Poor's, and the Securities and Exchange Commission. These public and private institutions have developed different mechanisms for reporting and evaluating financial information. In particular, various regulations have led to the standardization of the reporting of various financial information, such as income tax. Privately-created information such as credit ratings have also become important indicators of the financial health of debtors. As a result, financial transactions rely on the accuracy and availability of this type of information. Hence, the trustors, i.e., lenders, trust the institutions to provide correct and timely information needed to assess the risks associated with the transactions.

Some legal institutions enable the trustors to perform actions that reduce their vulnerability. For example, negotiability allows creditors to exit the debt relationship before the loan has come to maturity, and security gives the creditors claim over debtors' assets [4]. To the degree that the legal system as a whole can be trusted, these mechanisms make it possible for the lender to reduce her losses by moving the debt to a third party or by seizing a valuable asset. In essence, the trust for the credit rating depends on the legal system's ability to enforce the specific contract between the debtor and the creditor. We will discuss trust for the legal system in the next section.

Other financial institutions help to manage risk by grouping and evaluating multiple debts concurrently. For example, early banker's handbooks urged lenders to reduce their overall risk by making sure that the debtors come from different industries or geographic regions. This diversification of debt is meant to ensure that risks are uncorrelated and hence the amount of risk the lender is exposed to from one debtor is offset by the lower risk from another. On the other hand, securitization refers to the process of grouping loans into large pools, which can then be divided into smaller portfolios of similar risk and sold to other lenders. This process spreads the ownership of risk, makes it easier to sell the loans and create revenue for the lenders and other intermediaries. In essence, it allows risks to be defined more accurately for the securitized assets within the larger group. These mechanisms are different methods to manage risk, sometimes at the individual lender level and sometimes in the context of a large group of investments.

One of the institutions that underlies all financial transactions is the monetary system, which ensures that money exchanged in the transactions has value and this value is stable [4]. Lenders rely on the institutions that regulate the value of money and trust that the government behind a specific currency will not issue money at a rate that exceeds the rate of growth in the production of goods and services in the corresponding economy [8]. Finance in general involves a set of actors including bankers, brokers, traders, banks, insurance companies, hedge funds. These actors are involved in many different actions that go well beyond simple credit. An actor may serve one role (e.g., trustor) in one action, and another role (e.g., trustee) in another action, creating complex nested relationships. These actions are taken within the context of rules and regulations that describe which actions are possible by whom and when [5]. These rules can be quite complex, spanning markets, informal systems like the *hawala* system for international remittances, computer systems that link different investment banks, and the polity and laws of participating nations. As a result, understanding risk and trust in financial institutions requires an analysis of complex dependence relationships that go far beyond a simple pairwise relationship in the scope of a single transaction.

3.1.3 Trust in Legal and Political Institutions

In a study of trust in political institutions, Levi and Stoker [37] observe that trust for a political institution must be distinguished from the trust for those currently in power and trust for political parties. The distinction lies in whether the actions of a given organization or government are attributed to a specific person or people, or to the system in general. In particular, governmental institutions are expected to tell the truth to the people, and allow them to achieve autonomy, accumulate wealth and live free from fear and danger in their daily activities.

   We can consider the dependence on political institutions in two general areas. First, political institutions provide general expectations of risk in different aspects of their citizens' lives. When a system is successful in protecting its citizens against bad behavior in a social or economic area, this reduces the risk involved in interacting with trustees. In fact, trust between a trustor and the trustee involved in an economic transaction becomes more important in societies where formal support for credit is low because of civil conflict, widespread corruption, or ethnic discrimination [29]. Hence, when the system is trusted to safeguard the trustor against possible damage from the trustee, then the dependence of this transaction is shifted to the system. If the system works properly, possible problems will be resolved fairly and efficiently.

Fig. 3.2 Trust in legal institutions

Second, government officials hold power and authority. They are expected to uphold the responsibilities of their office and hence allow the system to perform its expected duties. One can expect that trustors' reliance on the system grows when there is no other basis for trust: no social context and prior experience with a specific trustee [37]. For example, in the absence of specific experience with a legal or political institution (Fig. 3.2), the individuals form their trust evaluation based on generalized expectations of the government. These expectations are driven by the norms of the social groups that individuals belong to. Overall, a difficult problem like: "how fair will the court hearing be?" is replaced with an easier one like "how much do I trust the government?".

Montinola [50] shows a specific instance of this phenomenon in the study of trust for local courts in Philippines. This study reveals that individuals with direct experience of the courts based their trust decisions on their individual experience. Those without any prior court experience rely on their overall trust for the government as represented by the president.

De Cremer and Tyler [10] study to which degree a micro-level observation, i.e., trust for the leader of an institution in power impacts the macro-level phenomenon, i.e., trust for the procedural fairness of a specific institution. The findings suggest that procedural fairness plays a role in trust evaluations when the trust in authority is high, but is not considered when the trust in authority is low. In this complex dependence relation, when trust in authority is low, procedural fairness does not matter. The institution is not trusted. Only when the authority is trusted, secondary concerns play a role.

Pagden [53] discusses how trust in institutions is deeply linked to social interactions that allow individuals to communicate and establish shared understanding and values. Culture can be considered as a set of social values that creates generalized expectations with regard to different institutions for a specific social group. Pagden argues that Spanish rulers of eighteenth Century Naples employed a number of tactics with the specific purpose of weakening the society and trust, to make it easier to rule it from afar. In particular, they created new hierarchies that undermined the existing authorities, new rules that made it for hard for different groups to establish trusting relationships, and different legal rules for different social groups that created suspicion and distrust towards the legal system. These actions ultimately lead to the destruction of trust towards various institutions and the steady collapse of trust within the society.

Yamagishi and Yamagishi [78] survey Japanese and American citizen and find that American citizens show more generalized trust towards others in their society. In contrast, Japanese citizens place a larger emphasis on the individual experience with the trustees. One explanation is that the Japanese society is more deeply embedded in social relations, making it less reliant on formal institutions overall for maintenance of trust.

How trust beliefs are formed by the trustors and what information they use to evaluate trust is discussed in detail in the Sect. 3.2. The examples above illustrate cases in which the trustor uses different criteria to decide whether to trust a trustee who is acting as part of a greater system. In such cases, the trustor's dependence is both on the specific trustee, e.g., the judge of a specific court, and the overall system that controls the actions available to the judge. In the absence of any information about the specific judge or the court system, the trust evaluation may depend on other external signals that are deemed relevant, such as perceptions about authority figures or cultural expectations.

3.1.4   Trust and Culture

It is not clear that we can define what culture is, but we can say that people live culturally. People are alike in their "cultural living" if they share the same values and ideas. People can be alike with respect to some values and different with respect to others. The more values they share, the more alike they are culturally [16].

As discussed in the previous section, culture allows people to develop common behavior patterns. These patterns can then be used to form expectations about how others will behave in the future [78] and what their intentions are. These are particularly useful in trust evaluations; those who are deemed to belong to one's own social group are expected to have positive intentions, which engenders cooperative behavior. On the other hand, those who are considered outside of one's social group are met with competitive and aggressive behavior [17].

There is a great deal of research in culture, with several dimensions of analysis. For example, one can consider whether the focus of attention is on individual achievements versus on overall harmony [51]. Nisbett points out the differences in eastern and western cultures in which individuals pay greater attention to either similarities between individuals or differences. In more individualistic cultures, people may pay more attention to reputation and have a higher level of trust towards individuals in general. Cultures that pay higher attention to relationships between people place a much higher importance in trust relationships based on prior experience [78].

Another approach due to anthropologist Mary Douglas [12] describes how society imposes control on individuals based on two dimensions. The group dimension measures how much people's lives are controlled by group expectations, i.e., whether they are individualistic or group-oriented. The grid dimension measures to which degree actions are structured around rules: whether individuals are expected to follow specific rules or if they are free to choose from a set of different behaviors. These two dimensions are a more detailed explanation of to which degree the individual's decisions depend on the group behavior and the specific rules of behavior.

Other approaches consider culture as a socially-constructed reality in which institutions themselves become actors and fulfill important functions. Objects have meaning because everyone believes that they do. Institutions become stores of knowledge which then regulate and control actions [77]. For example, a folk tale about a tsunami that appeared more than 1,000 years ago informed the residents about the correct course of action when the tsunami struck Miyatojima island in 2011 [30]. In such a view of culture, the expected behavior is deeply embedded in the cultural institutions that imbue meaning to specific signs, roles and situations [24].

Overall, the generalized trust expectations that are obtained from culture are not easy to formulate. Their main function is to provide a generalized expectation of trust that becomes especially important when interacting with a trustee from the same culture for the first time. If the trustor is very familiar with a trustee, she may no longer rely on expectations based on culture in her trust evaluations.

3.1.5 Trust in Teams

Research in team trust tries to identify to which degree trust in teams is different than the more generalized trust in the greater organizational context the team is operating in. A number of dimensions should be considered [18]. First, it is important to note whether the team members know each other before their interaction in the team. If the team members do not have any information about each other, then their trust is driven by some generalized notion of trust such as their own disposition, their similarity to each other (homophily) [46], and their expectations based on membership to specific groups or organizations. The second factor is whether the team members are expected to meet again. This means that the team members can obtain value from the ties that they form during the team activity, and that their social standing and reputation will be affected by their performance in the team. These aspects of team trust parallel the discussion of social trust in the scope of organizations.

One of the most important determinants of team performance is the access to information that is necessary for the team to complete its task [75]. Teams can rely on the members to provide easy access to information within the team, and at the same time facilitate access to information from outside of the team through team members' other ties. The types of ties team members have provide them with different advantages. For example, when the team task is complex, strong ties within the team are very useful. Strong ties in this context imply that team members share a common understanding of the problem and the organizational context. They can rely on each other to know specific terms and signs used, which reduces the cost of communication [27]. This is not true in the case of weak ties, which introduces uncertainty about the shared understanding of concepts. However, such ties may be useful to the team by giving it access to a more diverse information and talent pool.

Mechanisms that may impact trust in teams include the creation of an ingroup identity [18], which may lead to team cohesiveness, and expected competence and reciprocity within the team, but it may also lead to negative consequences. For example, cohesiveness may result in "group think" in which the members are unwilling to take the risk of disagreeing and challenging other's views. In other words, it may reduce the trust for conflicting and novel information in the team. On the flip side, the pyschological safety within the team may create the reverse effect [15] if the team members create a "culture of safety" in which one can openly act within the team without fear of sanctions. Overall, the small size of teams allows the creation of a set of shared values that can be beneficial or detrimental to trust depending on the situational aspects of team behavior and composition.

The structure of the team can play a crucial role in its success. A centralized communication system may be best for simple tasks. However, a distributed system works better for more complex tasks in which team members can undertake different subtasks. This reduces the need to communicate detailed information about the task, but creates a higher degree of dependence between team members. The dependence between team members can be much stronger than the more abstract sense of dependence on the organization, and can lead to an expectation of trust and the creation of an in-group identity. If the dependence on other members is moderate, then trust is more likely to develop [47]. At extremely high and low levels of dependence, team members are expected to be less willing to trust each other and take risks.

3.2 Trust as Belief of Trustworthiness (and Competence)

The largest literature on trust refers to trust as a belief: the trustor believes that the trustee can be trusted for a specific goal in a specific context. The trust can be interpersonal, interorganizational or intergroup [64] and include institutional factors. However, this type of study very often deals with trusting another person [62]. The emphasis is on identifying the specific conditions that require trust and the specific dimensions along which trust is evaluated. In the previous section, we studied the broader institutional context that impacts trust. In this section, we will discuss the trustworthiness component of trust, i.e., properties of the trustee that impact the perception of her trustworthiness.

Interpersonal trust has been studied in many different settings with specific emphasis on the characteristics of the trustor and the trustee that impact the degree to which the trustor will trust the trustee. In particular, the trustor's propensity to trust is one of the mediating factors for the trust belief. We will study this factor in detail in the next section. The specific characteristics of the trustee that are important for determining his trustworthiness differ greatly in the literature. In fact, McKnight and Chervany [44] review 60 articles and books on trust and list some of the most commonly used keywords for these characteristics. Based on a similar review, Mayer, Schoorman and Davis [41] offer additional keywords. Some of these are listed in Table 3.1. The first group shows keywords that talk about the warmth, friendliness and dependability of the trustee, which in some literature is split further into two groups as explained below. The second group refers to the abilities of the other. One way to think of these keywords is in a sentence describing why someone can be trusted: "Alice trusts Bob's integrity with respect to goal X" for the first group and "Alice trusts Bob's competence for goal X" for the second group.

Table 3.1 Examples of keywords from the literature used to describe the specific aspect or trait of another that makes them trustworthy or competent

Trustworthiness keywords
goodness, morality, benevolent, caring, showing concern, responsiveness, honesty, integrity, faith, dynamism, dependability, being careful, safe, shared understanding, personal attraction, availability, consistency, discreetness, fairness, loyalty, receptivity, promise fulfillment, intention to produce, altruism, autonomy, judgment, value congruence, persistence, fiduciary responsibility, tactfulness, sincerity, congeniality, accessibility

Competence keywords
competence, expertness, credibility, predictability, reliability, openness, open minded, timeliness, trial and error experience

While some keywords are quite common in the literature, the rest are used in specific contexts. Clearly many of these keywords are related to each other. One reason for this is the underlying ambiguity and variability of natural language. In addition, the true interpretation of the keyword depends on the goal. For some goals, certain keywords may have a very similar meaning, while for other goals, they may be very different. For example, being an expert in a task generally implies being competent in it. Being open-minded may or may not contribute to competence depending on the problem domain. However, using many different keywords to describe trustworthiness makes it hard to define what trust is and how it can be measured. Which properties can be tested? What instruments exist to test them? This is a topic of ongoing debate in the trust literature. In the area of interpersonal trust, a number of main classes of traits have been suggested with associated survey instruments to measure them. The objective is to find traits that are distinct from each other, and hence measure different aspects of the trust relationship.

3.2.1 Canonical Classification of Trust Beliefs

Mayer et al. [41] investigate interpersonal trust in an organizational setting. They propose three main groups:

Ability is a group of skills, competencies and characteristics that enable a party to have influence within some specific domain. Competence, expertness and credibility are good examples of keywords describing ability. Coleman [7] uses the term human capital as a good that is created by changes in people that bring about skills and capabilities that enable them to act in new ways. Hence, human capital is a factor that impacts a person's ability. Mayer et al. [41] discuss how ability of a person in a specific domain is impacted by her training, aptitude and experience in that domain.

Benevolence is the extent to which a trustee is believed to want to do good to the trustor, aside from an egocentric profit motive. For example, altruism, loyalty and good intentions contribute to benevolence.

Integrity involves the trustor's perception that the trustee adheres to a set of principles that the trustor finds acceptable. These principles can come from various sources such as value congruence, fairness, or morality.

We will often refer to this as the "canonical classification" of trust attributes. McKnight and Chervany [44, 45] add one more general dimension to the three proposed above: predictability that refers to which degree one's actions can be forecast in a specific situation. They also claim that openness, being careful, having a shared understanding, and personal attraction are orthogonal dimensions that are not explicitly covered by the above classification. Of these, shared understanding is closer to a social construct that is not a trait of the trustee, but a relationship between the trustor and the trustee. Openness and being careful can be considered as aspects of competence or ability in specific contexts. Predictability is an aspect that speaks to the behavior of the trustee, but its contribution to trustworthiness may depend greatly on the specific task. For example, predictability of behavior may signal competence for some tasks and good intentions in other tasks. We note that while many different classifications have been offered, there is general consensus that ability, benevolence and integrity are the main dimensions. In fact, McKnight and Chervany [44, 45] show that these three main categories are by far most commonly used in literature [2, 48, 36].

Schoorman et al. revisit this classification 10 years later [64]. They point out that the measures of trust obtained from a survey based on this classification produced mixed results in terms of internal consistency and reliability estimates. Different surveys were shown to be more effective in specific settings, while some surveys were later criticized to include only a few independent factors. The different settings used in the cited surveys generally refer to the relationship between employees and management in an organizational setting. However, the dependence relation between the trustor and the trustee in such cases can be impacted by institutional factors that go well beyond the trustworthines of the person. The dependence in such a case may not solely be on the trustee, but also on many other factors that we have described earlier.

All the work discussed so far aims to explain trust in social exchanges. On the other hand, trust in close relationships is often identified along different dimensions of predictability, dependability and faith [59]. Dependence in such relationships is more generalized and mainly targets aspects of benevolence and integrity.

Researchers have also studied when organizations can be considered trustworthy [50, 68]. Trust for an organization is generally based on perceived fairness of the rules and support provided to its members. Sitkin and Roth [68] discuss how legal remedies to establish trust generally impact the beliefs of the reliability of an organization, but do not impact their perception of the organizational values and the degree to which they are congruent with the trustor's values. Montinola [50] argues that values play a role when individuals observe members being treated with dignity, respect, politeness and sensitivity. Hence, while organizational rules speak to the overall competence of an organization, their execution signals its overall integrity and benevolence.

From the perspective of cognitive psychology, we first analyze the benevolence dimension. Research has shown that when people are told that they are interacting with individuals instead of computers (despite interacting with computers in both cases), a specific brain activation is observed [20]. This suggests that special significance is placed on interacting with someone who has his own beliefs and intentions. Thus, when interacting with someone, it is important to assess whether she is participating in a shared goal, such as in the case of a cooperative activity, or whether she has the same goal as us in the case of a competitive activity. In essence, judging the intentions of the trustee becomes very important in cooperative contexts. As a result, the notion of benevolence is a large factor, which coincides with positive intentions in the above taxonomy. In fact, this dimension has been studied in great detail in organizational contexts where cooperation is crucial. Studies have also proposed that shared intentionality, i.e., acting in accordance to shared goals, is a crucial factor for the development of social behavior [71]. According to this theory, understanding each other's goals and intentions is not sufficient for social and cultural artifacts to develop. Many social institutions require human beings to cooperate with each other in shared activities, playing different and complementary roles. This leads to shared beliefs that are required for the existence of institutions like money and government. The reality of these institutions is grounded in the collective beliefs of others.

3.2.2   Universal Dimensions: Trustworthiness and Competence

Social cognition research reveals that people use two main dimensions when forming impressions of other people. The first dimension assesses a person's intentions as warm (trustworthy, friendly, sincere, moral, communal) or not. This dimension is predicted by behaviors that indicate cooperation vs. competition, and public good vs. selfishness. The second dimension reflects opinions about the person's abilities (capability, skill, agency). One of the common signals used to make an inference about capability has to do with the person's status as well as his perceived facial dominance. Research shows that ability is evaluated differently than warmth. Individuals or social groups that are considered skillful but unfriendly, or friendly but incompetent, are not considered part of one's social group (neither are unfriendly and incompetent individuals for that matter). Unfriendly people are considered a threat, while incompetent people are simply pitied [17]. While this study comes from studies of impression formation in the short term, it correlates with the two main types of relationships classified by Uzzi [72] in the scope of economic exchanges between organizations: embedded friendship relationships and arm's length relationships based on the reputation of the trustee in the network. Other work uses the terms affect- and cognition-based trust in an organizational setting, which rely on factors like citizenship behavior for affect-based trust and professional credentials for cognition-based trust [42]. These two dimensions closely follow the warmth and competence dimensions from cognitive studies as well.

In essence, the warmth/competence taxonomy merges benevolence and integrity into a single dimension of trustworthiness. In other words, warmth summarizes whether one is considered a friend or foe. When one trusts another as a friend, she is likely to associate with that person many of the keywords offered at the top of Table 3.1. These keywords for the most part have an affective component. This affective element has been illustrated in many studies involving individuals playing various games with another [20]. Some studies have shown that individuals choose to punish an act perceived as unfair even though the punishment does not maximize their utility. This type of motive is considered pro-social where the punishment is altruistic and benefits others instead of oneself.

To sum up, trustworthiness and ability are two crucial factors considered when forming opinions of others mirroring integrity and ability from the taxonomy of Mayer et al. [41]. Benevolence is tied to the specific task at hand and the shared goals the individuals are pursuing in the given task. It is not clear whether benevolence is a distinct dimension for evaluating trustworthiness, as we will elaborate more in the next section.

3.2.3 Trustworthiness of Non-Human Actors

Trustworthiness traits are generally assigned to conscious beings or organizations containing human beings. However, research has examined whether non-human other entities can be trusted. Can robots be teammates? How do we trust automated systems to perform tasks? In particular, human interaction with automation can be framed as one of the following four main tasks [54]: information acquisition (e.g., getting sensor information about location), information analysis (e.g., getting

Fig. 3.3 Trustworthiness of non-human actors

directions from a system), decision selection (e.g., using expert systems for diagnostic help) and action implementation (e.g., sorting mail to different locations). Such automation is quickly becoming part of daily life. Early automation systems in manufacturing and flight control are still in existence today. On top of these, new examples of automation span a large range from the power grid infrastructure to mobile phones, and from intelligent information agents like Siri® to many different types of sensor-based devices.

Research shows that people tend to associate human-like attributes to non-human actors, to the point that departure from human-like behavior creates an unnerving effect (often called the "uncanny valley" in which the strong resemblance to humans is uncomfortable) [40]. Reeves and Nass [58] show that humans project a social identity on media and technologies that offer social cues. People talk to their devices, and show an emotional connection towards them; they try to be polite to technology that assists them and get angry at technology that does not work properly. As a result, many non-human entities can be considered as trustees. Literature in human factors design investigates what type of traits are associated with non-human trustees.

Hancock et al. [25] discuss whether robots can be trusted as teammates. Here "robot" is a general term given to any system that automates actions generally carried out by humans. The authors argue that our understanding of what a robot is and what it is capable of is shaped by examples in popular culture, and our expectations of behavior based on these. Hancock et al. [26] show that robot performance-based factors (e.g., predictability, reliability) and robot attributes (e.g., proximity, adaptability) are the largest contributors to trust in human-robot interactions. These can be construed as trustworthiness attributes of robots (Fig. 3.3).

Lee and See [36] discuss how trust in automation should be calibrated to the capability of the trusted system. For example, over-reliance on sensors can lead to negative consequences if the pilots fail to question the readings of faulty sensors in time to prevent a plane crash. Lee and See identify three "traits" that impact the trust in an automation system. The first, *performance*, describes what the automation does and how reliable it is. In the canonical classification of trust attributes, this corresponds to the ability of the trustee. The second, *process*, describes the degree to which the automation's algorithms are appropriate for achieving the operator's goals. This is similar to the definition of integrity, but is not associated with specific values. It describes the fit of the system for the specific problem.

The final component, *purpose*, refers to the algorithms and operations that govern the behavior of the automation and encode the original intent of its creators. In popular culture, this is sometimes discussed as whether a robot can be designed to do no harm and to which degree this can be codified in an algorithm [25]. This component resembles benevolence, but the question becomes whether the system is perceived as having intentionality. Does the intelligent agent participate in a shared goal with the trustor? Without a shared goal, can one talk about intentions, or is the robot behaving according to some specific design? Without these attributions, people seem to treat machines differently than other people [20]. In fact, neurological studies indicate that different parts of the brain are involved when forming opinions about humans (which tends to activate the medial prefrontal cortex (mPFC)) vs. inanimate objects (which does not involve significant activation of the mPFC) [49].

In support of the point that robots cannot be team-members, Groom and Nass [22] argue that robots lack a mental model and a sense of self. The values or the intent of the robot may not be visible to the human team-member. As a result, robots will not be accepted as trustworthy teammates. The authors argue that most research involving trust in automation concentrates on situations that do not involve high risk and human stress. The dependence on robots in these systems is not critical, but useful. Research suggests that people may choose to delegate a task to a robot or automation only if they perceive their own ability to perform the task to be low [39]. These results indicate that while robots or automation in general can be considered trustworthy, but this construct is not identical to that for human trustees. Hence, care must be taken when applying results from human teams to situations involving non-human entities.

Overall, this large body of work is based on the assumption that the trustworthiness belief is described by different and possibly orthogonal traits of the trustee. To which degree these traits are important is determined by the trustor's goals. While the traits can be put in specific categories as described above, the interpretation of each category is still specific to the given context. In fact, we can consider these traits as specific aspects of the dependence of the trustor on the trustee. For example, a trustor loaning money to another is dependent on the trustee's integrity and capability to pay it back. A trustor trying to escape in a disaster is relying on the ability of the trustee to provide correct and timely information. We will discuss trust in information shortly. Furthermore, the trustee is trusted not to withhold information and work to help the trustor. As a result, we can treat all these keywords as describing the dependency aspect of context in specific situations. Their large number represents the large variety of contexts in which trust becomes an important concept.

3.2.4 Formation of Trust Beliefs

Trust is not a static belief; it changes over time as a function of various stimuli. The way in which individuals form beliefs about trustworthiness of others has been predominantly studied through surveys, as well as through behavioral experiments involving various types of investment games. The survey method tends to focus on the long-term development of trust. The development of social relationships typically takes a long time, and has long-term effects on the success of the participants. On the other hand, economic games typically involve people with no prior knowledge of each other, and involve the shorter term effects of reciprocity and processing of signals related to trustworthiness. These studies are used to understand how people react to different incentives and sanctions as well as by cognitive psychologists to understand the social cognition of others' trustworthiness.

In social psychology, the emphasis is on understanding how individuals form beliefs of trustworthiness as a function of their interactions with another person or entity. In the absence of prior interactions, generalized expectations of trust are substituted. These expectations can come from many different sources. For example, the social, cultural or organizational context can provide such clues. A person's role can be used to infer trust about their abilities, like trusting an engineer, based on information about institutions that provide the necessary education [34]. Social groups and culture also provide important clues, depending on to which degree the individual is part of them, as well as how stable and trusted they are. In social exchanges, recommendations from a trusted third party can help establish expectations of trust.

Individuals also substitute simpler heuristics for evaluating trustworthiness, such as appearance or homophily [46], i.e., similarity to self in some aspect. These heuristics are especially active when there is no firsthand or other contextual information about the trustee. As one gains experience with the trustee, it is expected that trust evaluation is shaped increasingly by one's personal evaluation of the trustee [6, 37, 50, 64].

A common topic of study is the investigation of to which degree these other factors continue to impact trust evaluation in the presence of firsthand knowledge [6]. A personality trait called propensity to trust or disposition moderates the level of trust in all situations. The propensity varies from trustor to trustor, and can be measured by Rotter's Interpersonal Trust Scale [60]. Individuals with high propensity to trust are not more gullible than low propensity people [61], and propensity is not correlated with intellect [23]. However, high propensity individuals are more likely to be viewed as trustworthy by others [35].

From the perspective of cognitive psychology, researchers study how individuals form impressions about the intent of others by studying the brain activity of individuals participating in various economic games [1]. When analysing another's intent, people tend to focus primarily on their behavior. Even though the behavior of others is significantly influenced by the specific situations in which the behavior is observed, people tend to generalize their observations to many others. When forming opinions about another's expected behavior based on second-hand information, the more distinctive the information is, the more valuable it is. If Alice hears that Bob has done something, for this to be a useful information about Bob, two things should be true: Bob's action should not be common to everyone and Bob should perform this action consistently over time and over different situations. Opinions formed by second-hand information such as those that come from reputation can be persistent. Individuals were first told information about others and then played a trust game with those others, getting firsthand behavioral information [11]. In these experiments, the initial impressions were more influential than the actual behavior to decide to which degree the other can be trusted. This indicates that while actions have an impact on impressions of trustworthiness, the impact may not be as strong as that of reputational information. A great deal of firsthand behavioral information may be needed to overwrite such impressions, such as those developed through long-term social interactions.

The impact of faces on forming opinions of others has attracted a great deal of interest. Recognizing one's friend or foe quickly provides a unique evolutionary advantage, and as a result humans have specialized brain regions for the processing of faces [70]. Furthermore, people tend to make very quick assessment of faces without much cognitive effort; a 33 ms exposure to a face is sufficient for them to decide whether the face is trustworthy or not [76]. Regions of brain that are responsible for emotion and decision making are activated when a person looks at negatively perceived, i.e., untrustworthy faces. The emotional reactions aroused by the processing of faces, friend or foe, allow people to direct their attention to likely friends and stay away from harm. An even more interesting finding is that people tend to agree on their social judgments of the faces [76]. Similar to the case of second-hand information, individuals who have been shown faces with a specific trustworthiness valence played a trust game. In the future games, the individuals continued to rely on the impression formed by the faces, in some studies more than the actual behavior they observed [74]. In other studies, the valence assigned to faces changed as a function of observed behavior [67].

Firsthand experiences, especially those obtained from observing the behavior of others form a basis for judging their trustworthiness. The studies discussed earlier aim to understand how much people rely on observed behavior in judging others' future behavior. In the case of evaluations based on faces, the trustor is reconciling two different systems of evaluation: memory based and effortful in the case of processing behavioral information vs. perceptual, emotional and cheap to evaluate in the case of facial information. In fact, the experiments show that people rely on these two evaluations with different weights, perceptual evaluations playing an important and lasting role. In the case of second-hand information, the trustor chooses between the reliability of her own observations and the trustworthiness of the source of second-hand information. Even when the information is presented without citing a specific source, the trustor can substitute her trust for the examiner as a way to judge the credibility of the information source. In both cases, the trustor learns from firsthand experiences, but other sources have a significant impact in trust evaluations.

A recent study [6] aims to understand how firsthand experiences are integrated into the initial trustworthiness beliefs obtained from facial impressions. The model that best explains the observed behavior suggests that first impressions are used as a lens in which the feedback obtained from firsthand experience is evaluated. If the evidence confirms the initial impressions, it is believed more easily. Otherwise, it has a limited effect and the learning is much slower. This process changes the initial impressions, which in turn has an effect on the processing of future evidence.

Studies also elaborate on the differences between trustworthiness and ability judgments. The common signals used to make an inference about ability have to do with the status of the other person as well as his perceived facial dominance [17]. Research also sheds light on how trustworthiness and ability impact behavior at the cognitive level [17]. Trustworthiness perceived as warmth and friendship is judged before competence. As a result, trustworthiness evaluations carry more weight in both emotional and behavioral reactions. The judgment of friendship is easily impacted by negative evidence that is considered diagnostic of a problem, whereas positive evidence does not carry equal weight. For example, an untrusworthy person may act trustworthy for the purpose of deception. As far as competence is concerned, positive evidence is more diagnostic. More positive evidence imply higher level of competence. If somebody is considered competent, small errors are more easily forgiven. These two dimensions also apply to group based behavior. People from the same social groups tend to find each other friendly and competent. People considered to be from different social groups are viewed as unfriendly and incompetent.

Another recent emphasis is on understanding how emotions impact trust. These findings show that emotions from unrelated events can be carried over to later evaluations of trustees [13]. Emotions with positive valence like happiness increase trust, while emotions with negative valence like anger decrease trust. This is specifically true if the emotion is considered to be causally related to another person such as anger and gratitude. However, emotions that originate from internal evaluations, such as pride and guilt, do not impact trust evaluations as much. Furthermore, in-group and out-group evaluations of trust are linked to emotions associated with specific situational dangers posed by these groups [9]. For example, a threat to physical safety evokes fear while an obstacle to a desired outcome results in anger.

Overall, beliefs of trustworthiness are formed as a function of information about trustees, the social groups that they belong to and the firsthand experience with them. The impressions formed about another person through descriptions, recommendations, or by their facial and other physical attributes; play an important role in trustworthiness beliefs. In general, friendship relationships tend to imply benevolence and integrity. However, capability is evaluated along a separate axis. Network status, in particular, is an important signal used to infer capability.

3.3   Trust in Information

So far, we have concentrated on the trust a person has for other entities such as people, institutions or even machines. This type of trust is generally framed as trusting an entity to accomplish a task. In these examples, the trustor is dependent on the trustee to perform a specific action, e.g., to participate in a transaction or to provide information, before the action happens. We refer to this concept as trust for actions. A parallel literature examines how the trustor may trust information that is provided by a specific source. In this case, information is already provided and now the trustor needs to decide whether the information can be trusted. We will refer to this concept as trusting information. In this section, we examine how trust for information and trust for actions differ.

Information trust is by no means a recent concern. For example, the topic has been studied in great detail in the field of law, where it is crucial to judge whether testimony provided in court is correct and can be trusted. How do we trust information provided by different witnesses, especially when they conflict each

Fig. 3.4   Trust in information

other? What type of uniform criteria can be established for this purpose? However, the topic has gained particular importance with the explosion of information available online. All individuals and organizations have become potential publishers of data, providing data with an ever-increasing speed. What are the appropriate methods to judge trust of online information? In addition, automation research addresses trust in information provided by sensors and information analysis tools. In this case, the trustor has to decide whether to trust the information provided by a specific source (Fig. 3.4).

Starting with the law literature [65], almost all literature on information trust makes a distinction between two concepts: credibility of the witness and credibility of their testimony. Competence refers to the expertness of the witness or the information source in the specific information domain and their mental ability. Trustworthiness refers to the possible motives of the witness and his character. The source credibility depends on factors like (borrowing from the law literature): the person's character, demeanor, past history with the law, his physical and situational abilities to observe what he is reporting, whether he has something to gain by what he is reporting and so on. The second dimension looks at the credibility of the testimony which generally means the believability of the story he is providing, whether it corroborates or conflicts the testimony given by other witnesses. This dimension refers to the message, not the source.

These two factors can both significantly impact information trust: a seemingly unbelievable piece of information can be trusted if it comes from a very trusted source: for example, the recent surprising research finding that passed rigorous peer review. A highly believable piece of information from an untrusted source may also be trusted to some degree. A frequently used term in this case is "trust but verify". People may trust information that generally agrees with their viewpoint [66] due to a well-known phenomenon called confirmation bias. A person's familiarity with a topic may make them better at identifying the more credible sources [3], but at the same time predispose her to reject sources that provide an alternate point of view. Similarly, people unfamiliar with a topic may rely solely on sources that they consider trustworthy, despite lacking the skills necessary to identify their reliability properly.

Table 3.2 Examples of constructs (keywords) used to evaluate information trust

Information trust keywords
truthfulness, believability, trustworthiness, objectivity, reliability, validity, stability, freshness, timeliness, relevance, appropriateness

As a result, trust in information incorporates two distinct concepts, the trustor's trust in the information source and her trust in the information content, into a single trust evaluation. This is a departure from trust in actions, where the trustor is dependent on the trustee to accomplish a certain task. In the case of information, the trustor is also dependent on herself to interpret the information. Often, information trust and credibility are used interchangeably, but sometimes credibility is attached only to the message content. For clarity, we will use the term information trust as a construct that includes both the trust in the source and the message content.

Hilligoss and Rieh [28] report on previous work in this field and their own empirical study. To explain information trust, one has to first identify the goal of the trustor. Which aspects of the information are crucial to trusting the information? Hence, the construct used to evaluate information must be defined. Researchers give truthfulness, believability, trustworthiness, objectivity and reliability as examples of such constructs. Other examples are validity and stability of information [32]. The meanings of these constructs are tied to the decision context. For example, reliability of the information may be due to its freshness, timeliness, relevance, and appropriateness for a specific task. We summarize these constructs in Table 3.2. Once the construct is defined, both the trustworthiness of the source and the information are evaluated accordingly.

Studies identify factors that are used to evaluate the credibility of sources. The source of information can be a person such as a witness in a trial, an automated system such as a sensor showing the malfunction of a car component, a map application suggesting a route to drive to a specific location, or an online site providing information. When judging the trustworthiness of online sites, the problem is that the site may not be known to the user in advance. In essence, the site may contain misinformation with the intention to harm or to advertise a specific point of view. This topic has been studied a great deal in the field of health, due to public health concerns raised by incorrect and possibly harmful information available on the Internet. For health information, people are recommended to use sites that are expert in the topic, provide current information, and do not have competing interests in providing the information [3]. For example, a site backed by a drug company may overemphasize the benefit of some drugs or drugs in general. However, if it is not possible to evaluate sites along these axes, then other signs are needed to infer trustworthiness of the sources.

Research also investigates what types of cues are frequently used by people to judge trustworthiness of sites. Often, the visual appeal of a site presenting information is viewed positively. Design that is attractive, is personalized to a specific audience, has a clear layout, uses relevant illustrations, and employs clear and simple language all impacts trustworthiness assessment positively. Pop up ads, broken links, busy layout, small print, too much text, corporate look and feel, lack of navigation aids, and poor search functionality all impact the trustworthiness evaluation negatively. Similar to processing of faces, factors obtained purely from visual cues are processed very quickly and can help form first impressions for unknown sites. These surface characteristics fall into general categories of appearance/presentation, usability/interface design, and organization of information. These first impressions can be very strong factors in deciding whether to explore a site at all [3, 66].

The other factors that are used to judge source trustworthiness are either obtained from direct experience with the site or from generalized expectations about the specific media that the site belongs to: blogs, Wikipedia, newspapers and so on [66]. This is similar to the impact of institutions in forming impressions. Such impressions are replaced by the trustor's perceptions of the site as she interacts with it. Sources are generally interpreted for their expertise or competence in the specific area. Other factors such as objectivity and relevance to the given task can also be used in this evaluation. People also report that they trust sites that provide information from people like themselves, in essence making it easy to identify with the information provided in these sites. Other endorsements are also used to infer trustworthiness beliefs. The endorsements may come from friends and colleagues, can be references and links to the site from other trusted sites [69], or signs displayed on the site like certificates. These endorsements are a form of second-hand knowledge that has been shown to be an important factor in forming trust beliefs.

Petty and Cacioppo [55, 56] identify two information processing methods used by individuals: systematic and heuristic. Systematic processing is effortful, such as judging the veracity and objectivity of information. For systematic processing to happen, the trustor must not have a high cognitive load. However, even in cases where cognitive resources are available, people often use a less costly approach based on heuristics. Site characteristics, such as visual appeal, for example are heuristics that can be used in place of more systematic evaluation. Kahneman calls this substitution [31]: instead of answering the costly query of whether the information provided by a source is believable, the person substitutes a simpler question: does the site look and feel credible? The heuristic approach generally looks for coherence of signs and engages the systematic evaluation only when there is a perceived need. Using heuristics saves cognitive energy, but may lead to incorrect decisions as in the case of confirmation bias. We note a parallel with the processing of warmth and competence dimensions for people. Evaluating warmth, friendliness and trustworthiness is faster and less effortful than deciding on competence. Hence, perceptions of the source along the "warmth" dimension given by visual cues and the availability of relatable material have a large impact on information trust. For example, studies show the importance of factors like speed of response, listing a physical address, and including photos of an organization. Similarly, in a study, the tendency of pilots to follow the advice of a system increased when the aid included detailed pictures [52]. These factors all relate to the trustworthiness of the site along the first dimension [19].

In addition to considering the processes like heuristic and systematic evaluation of relevant factors, information search and evaluation is viewed as a continuous and iterative process. Pirolli and Fu [57] introduced a cognitive framework for information foraging. According to this framework, as information seekers visit multiple sites, they build a mental model of topics and concepts relevant to the current information task. This model also incorporates the relationships between topics and concepts. The trustor's mental model impacts how new information and the sites providing this information are viewed. This short-term model of information and concepts helps the trustor judge the relevance of information. Sillence et al. [66] propose a similar process for information trust, in which trustors sift through a large number of sites using heuristic criteria to decide on a number of candidate sites to analyze. These sites are then evaluated using more systematic criteria, such as more careful reading of material and interaction.

All of these examples come from tasks in which the trustor is seeking information passively from different sites. Similar to a trial, as more evidence is obtained that corroborates the information, it is more likely to be believed. In essence, as more information is obtained, the trustor's belief about which information can be trusted changes. New studies concentrate on other signals obtained from aggregate behavior of people. For example, crowd-sourcing is quickly becoming a valid way to solve problems by asking a question to many untrusted sources with the assumption that the consensus of the crowd will provide the most trusted information. We will discuss this application area in more detail in the next section. Saavedraa et al. [63] show that the amount of synchrony between people corroborating the same message can be a valuable signal of information credibility. Furthermore, they show that some people are able to correctly process such information even in highly stressful situations.

The relationship between source trust and the trustor's evaluation of the message is also discussed in the social psychology literature. If the trustor is able to understand whether the information is correct or not, then there is little dependence on the trustworthiness of the source. When searching for information, people frequently consult others. In an organizational setting, knowledge falls into two main categories: explicit information that can be documented, and tacit information such as know-how that is not easy to share. Often, tacit information is obtained from shared experiences. It incorporates implicit assumptions that are hard to transmit as information. Levin and Cross [38] investigate two types of source trust: competence and benevolence. They show that competence trust is more important to obtain useful knowledge when that knowledge is tacit. If the knowledge is explicit, then the trustor can easily get the information themselves. Benevolence, however, always matters. "If people think someone is out to harm them, they will be suspicious of everything that person says, no matter how simple or complex" [38]. Hence, the nature of information is part of the trust construct used to evaluate trust.

References

1. D. Ames, S. Fiske, A. Todorov, Impression formation: a focus on others intents, in *The Oxford Handbook of Social Neuroscience*, ed. by J. Decety, J. Cacioppo (Oxford University Press, New York, 2011), pp. 419–433
2. B. Barber, *The Logic and Limits of Trust* (Rutgers University Press, New Brunswick, 1983)
3. B.R. Bates, S. Romina, R. Ahmed, D. Hopson, The effect of source credibility on consumer's perceptions of the quality of health information on the internet. Med. Inform. Internet Med. **31**(1), 45–52 (2006)
4. B.G. Carruthers, Trust and credit, in *Whom Can We Trust? How Groups, Networks and Institutions Make Trust Possible*, ed. by K.S. Cook, M. Levi, R. Hardin (Russell Sage Foundation, New York, 2009), pp. 219–248
5. B.G. Carruthers, J.-C. Kim, The sociology of finance. Annu. Rev. Sociol. **37**(1), 239–259 (2011)
6. L.J. Chang, B.B. Doll, M. van 't Wout, M.J. Frank, A.G. Sanfey, Seeing is believing: Trustworthiness as a dynamic belief. Cogn. Psychol. **61**(2), 87–105 (2010)
7. J.S. Coleman, Social capital in the creation of human capital. Am. J. Sociol. Supplement: Organizations and Institutions: Sociological and Economic Approaches to the Analysis of Social Structure, **94**, S95–S120 (1988)
8. J.S. Coleman, *Foundations of Social Theory* (Harvard University Press, Cambridge, 1990)
9. C.A. Cottrell, S.L. Neuberg, Different emotional reactions to different groups: a sociofunctional threat-based approach to "prejudice". J. Personal. Soc. Psychol. **88**(5), 770–789 (2005)
10. D.D. Cremer, T.R. Tyler, The effects of trust and procedural justice on cooperation. J. Appl. Psychol. **92**, 639–649 (2007)
11. M.R. Delgado, R.H. Frank, E.A. Phelps, Perceptions of moral character modulate the neural systems of reward during the trust game. Nat. Neurosci. **8**, 1611–1618 (2005)
12. M. Douglas, *Risk and Blame: Essays in Cultural Theory* (Routledge, New York, 1992)
13. J.R. Dunn, M.E. Schweitzer, Feeling and believing: the influence of emotion on trust. J. Personal. Soc. Psychol. **88**(5), 736–748 (2005)
14. D. Easley, J. Kleinberg, *Networks, Crowds, and Markets: Reasoning About a Highly Connected World* (Cambridge University Press, New York, 2010)
15. A. Edmondson, Psychological safety and learning behavior in work teams. Adm. Sci. Q. **44**(2), 350–383 (1999)
16. D.L. Everett, *Language: The Cultural Tool* (Vintage, New York, 2012)
17. S.T. Fiske, A.J. Cuddy, P. Glick, Universal dimensions of social cognition: warmth and competence. Trends Cogn. Sci. **11**(2), 77–83 (2007)
18. M. Foddy, T. Yamagishi, Group-based trust, in *Whom Can We Trust? How Groups, Networks and Institutions Make Trust Possible*, ed. by K.S. Cook, M. Levi, R. Hardin (Russell Sage Foundation, New York, 2009), pp. 17–41
19. B. Fogg, J. Marshall, O. Laraki, A. Osipovich, C. Varma, N. Fang, What makes web sites credible? a report on a large quantitative study, in *Proceedings of CHI Conference on Human Factors in Computing Systems*, Seattle, 2001, pp. 61–68
20. C.D. Frith, T. Singer, The role of social cognition in decision making. Philos. Trans. R. Soc. Lon. Ser. B Biol. Sci. **363**(1511), 3875–3886 (2008)
21. M. Granovetter, Economic action and social structure: the problem of embeddedness. Am. J. Sociol. **91**, 481–510 (1985)
22. V. Groom, C. Nass, Can robots be teammates? Benchmarks in human robot teams. Interact. Stud. **8**(3), 483–500 (2007)
23. M.B. Gurtman, Trust, distrust and interpersonal problems: a circumplex analysis. J. Personal. Soc. Psychol. **62**, 989–1002 (1992)
24. E.T. Hall, *The Silent Language* (Anchor, Garden City, 1973)
25. P.A. Hancock, D.R. Billings, K.E. Schaefer, Can you trust your robot? Ergon. Des.: Q. Hum. Factors Appl. **19**(3), 24–29 (2011)

26. P.A. Hancock, D.R. Billings, K.E. Schaefer, J.Y. Chen, E.J. de Visser, P. Parasurama, A meta-analysis of factors affecting trust in human-robot interaction. Hum. Factors **53**(5), 517–527 (2011)
27. M.T. Hansen, The search-transfer problem: the role of weak ties in sharing knowledge across organization subunits. Adm. Sci. Q. **44**(1), 82–111 (1999)
28. B. Hilligoss, S.Y. Rieh, Developing a unifying framework of credibility assessment: construct, heuristics and interaction in context. Inf. Process. Manag. **44**, 1467–1484 (2008)
29. P.T. Hoffman, G. Postel-Vinay, J.-L. Rosenthal, The role of trust in the long-run development of french financial markets, in *Whom Can We Trust? How Groups, Networks and Institutions Make Trust Possible*, ed. by K.S. Cook, M. Levi, R. Hardin (Russell Sage Foundation, New York, 2009), pp. 249–285
30. J. Holguin-Veras, Japan's 1,000-year-old warning (2012), http://articles.latimes.com/2012/mar/11/opinion/la-oe-holguin-veras-tsunami-20120311, Mar 2012. Accessed 14 Oct 2012
31. D. Kahneman, *Thinking, Fast and Slow* (Farrar, Straus and Giroux, New York, 2011)
32. K. Kelton, K.R. Fleischmann, W.A. Wallace, Trust in digital information. J. Am. Soc. Inf. Sci. Technol. **59**, 363–374 (2008)
33. P. Kollock, E.R. Braziel, How not to build an online market: the sociology of market microstructure, in *Advances in Group Processes: Social Psychology of the Workplace*, ed. by S.R. Thye, E.J. Lawler (Elsevier Science, New York, 2006)
34. R.M. Kramer, Trust and distrust in organizations: emerging perspectives, enduring questions. Annu. Rev. Psychol. **50**, 569–598 (1999)
35. M. Kukichi, Y. Watanabe, T. Yamasishi, Judgment accuracy of other's trustworthiness and general trust: an experimental study. Jpn. J. Exp. Soc. Psychol. **37**, 23–36 (1996)
36. J.D. Lee, K.A. See, Trust in automation: designing for appropriate reliance. Hum. Factors **46**(1), 50–80 (2004)
37. M. Levi, L. Stoker, Political trust and trustworthiness. Annu. Rev. Pol. Sci. **3**, 475–507 (2000)
38. D.Z. Levin, R. Cross, The strength of weak ties you can trust: the mediating role of trust in effective knowledge transfer. Acad. Manag. J. **50**(11), 1477–1490 (2002)
39. S. Lewandowsky, M. Mundy, G. Tan, The dynamics of trust: Comparing humans to automation. J. Exp. Psychol. Appl. **6**, 104–123 (2000)
40. K.F. MacDorman, H. Ishiguro, The uncanny advantage of using androids in cognitive and social science research. Interact. Stud. **7**(3), 297–337 (2006)
41. R.C. Mayer, F. Schoorman, J. Davis, An integrative model of organizational trust. Acad. Manag. Rev. **20**(3), 709–734 (1995)
42. D.J. McAllister, Affect and cognition based trust as foundations for interpersonal cooperation in organizations. Acad. Manag. J. **38**(1), 24–59 (1995)
43. D. McFadden, Free markets and fettered consumers. Am. Econ. Rev. **96**, 5–29 (2006)
44. D.H. McKnight, N.L. Chervany, The meanings of trust. Technical report, Michigan State University, 1996
45. D.H. McKnight, N.L. Chervany, What trust means in e-commerce customer relationships: an interdisciplinary conceptual typology. Int. J. Electron. Commer. **6**, 35–59 (2001)
46. M. McPherson, L. Smith-Lovin, J.M. Cook, Birds of a feather: homophily in social networks. Annu. Rev. Sociol. **27**(1), 415 (2001)
47. D. Meyerson, K.E. Weick, R.M. Kramer, Swift-trust and temporary groups, in *Trust in Organizations: Frontiers of Theory and Research*, ed. by R.M. Kramer, T.R. Tyler (Sage Publications, Thousand Oaks, 1996), pp. 166–195
48. A.K. Mishra, Organizational response to crisis, in *Trust in Organizations: Frontiers of Theory and Research*, ed. by R.M. Kramer, T.R. Tyler (Sage Publications, Thousand Oaks, 1996), pp. 261–287
49. J.P. Mitchell, C.N. Macrae, M.R. Banaji, Forming impressions of people versus inanimate objects: social-cognitive processing in the medial prefrontal cortex. NeuroImage **26**(1), 251–257 (2005)

50. G.R. Montinola, Proxies and experience as bases of trust in courts, in *Whom Can We Trust? How Groups, Networks and Institutions Make Trust Possible*, ed. by K.S. Cook, M. Levi, R. Hardin (Russell Sage Foundation, New York, 2009), pp. 286–307
51. R. Nisbett, K. Peng, I. Choi, A. Norenzayan, Culture and systems of thought: holistic versus analytic cognition. Psychol. Rev. **108**(2), 291–310 (2001)
52. J.J. Ockerman, Over-reliance issues with task-guidance systems, in *Proceedings of the Human Factors and Ergonomics Society 43rd Annual Meeting*, Houston, 1999, pp. 1192–1196
53. A. Pagden, The destruction of trust and its consequences in eighteenth century naples, in *Trust: Making and Breaking Cooperative Relations*, ed. by D. Gambetta (Blackwell, New York, 1988)
54. R. Parasuraman, T. Sheridan, C. Wickens, A model for types and levels of human interaction with automation. IEEE Trans. Syst. Man Cybern. Part A: Syst. Hum. **30**(3), 286–297 (2000)
55. R.E. Petty, J.T. Cacioppo, *Attitude and Persuasion: Classic and Comtemporary Approaches* (Westview Press, Boulder, 1981)
56. R.E. Petty, J.T. Cacioppo, The elaboration likelihood model of persuasion. Adv. Exp. Soc. Psychol. **19**, 123–205 (1986)
57. P. Pirolli, W.-T. Fu, Snif-act: a model of information foraging on the world wide web, in *User Modeling 2003*, ed. by P. Brusilovsky, A.T. Corbett, F. de Rosis (Springer, London/New York, 2003), p. 146
58. B. Reeves, C. Nass, *The Media Equation: How People Treat Computers, Television, and New Media Like Real People and Places* (Center for the Study of Language and Inf, 2003, Stanford, California)
59. J. Rempel, J. Holmes, M. Zanna, Trust in close relationships. J. Personal. Soc. Psychol. **49**(1), 95–112 (1995)
60. J.B. Rotter, A new scale for the measurement of interpersonal trust. J. Personal. **35**, 651–665 (1967)
61. J.B. Rotter, Interpersonal trust, trustworthiness, and gullibility. Am. Psychol. **35**, 1–7 (1980)
62. D.M. Rousseau, S.B. Sitkin, R.S. Burt, C. Camerer, Not so different after all: a cross-discipline view of trust. Acad. Manag. Rev. **23**, 393–404 (1998)
63. S. Saavedraa, K. Hagerty, B. Uzzi, Synchronicity, instant messaging, and performance among financial traders. Proc. Natl. Acad. Sci. (PNAS), 1018462108v1–201018462 (2011)
64. F.D. Schoorman, R.C. Mayer, J.H. Davis, An integrative model of organizational trust: past, present and future. Acad. Manag. Rev. **32**(2), 344–354 (2007)
65. D.A. Schum, J.R. Morris, Assessing the competence and credibility of human resources of intelligence evidence: contributions from law and probability. Law Probab. Risk **6**, 247–274 (2007)
66. E. Sillence, P. Briggs, P.R. Harris, L. Fishwick, How do patients evaluate and make use of online health information? Soc. Sci. Med. **64**, 1853–1862 (2007)
67. T. Singer, S.J. Kiebel, J.S. Winston, R.J. Dolan, C.D. Frith, Brain responses to the acquired moral status of faces. Neuron **41**(4), 653–662 (2004)
68. S.B. Sitkin, N.L. Roth, Explaining the limited effectiveness of legalistic "remedies" for trust/distrust. Organ. Sci. **4**(3), 367–392 (1993)
69. K.J. Stewart, Y. Zhang, Effects of hypertext links on trust transfer, in *Proceedings of ICEC*, Pittsburgh, 2003, pp. 235–239
70. A. Todorov, N.N. Oosterhof, Modeling social perception of faces. IEEE Signal Process. Mag. **28**, 117 (2011)
71. M. Tomasello, M. Carpenter, J. Call, T. Behne, H. Moll, Understanding and sharing intentions: the origins of cultural cognition. Behav. Brain Sci. **28**(5), 675–91; discussion 691–735 (2005)
72. B. Uzzi, The sources and consequences of embeddedness for the economic performance of organizations: the network effect. Am. Sociol. Rev. **61**, 674–698 (1996)
73. B. Uzzi, A social network's changing statistical properties and the quality of human innovation. J. Phys. A: Math. Theor. **41**, 224023 (12pgs) (2008)
74. M. van 't Wout, A.G. Sanfey, Friend or foe: the effect of implicit trustworthiness judgments in social decision-making. Cognition **108**(3), 796–803 (2008)

75. D.M. Wegner, Transactive memory: a contemporary analysis of the group mind, in *Theories of Group Behavior*, ed. by B. Mullen, G. Goethals (Springer, New York, 1986)
76. J. Willis, A. Todorov, First impressions: making up your mind after 100 ms exposure to a face. Psychol. Sci. **17**, 592–598 (2006)
77. R. Wuthnow, J.D. Hunter, A. Bergesen, E. Kurzweil, *Cultural Analysis: The Work of Peter L. Berger, Mary Douglas, Michel Foucault and Jurgen Habermas* (Routledge and Kegan Paul, Boston/London, 1984)
78. T. Yamagishi, M. Yamagishi, Trust and commitment in the United States and Japan. Motiv. Emot. **18**, 129–166 (1994)

Chapter 4
Trust in Computing

Trust is a very frequently used term in Computer Science. In this chapter, we will review some of the different contexts in which it is used and draw parallels when applicable with social cognitive trust constructs. The computing literature frequently uses the term trust to describe an institution that is designed to make hardware and software more reliable so that people will choose them to communicate with each other, store personal information, find information and to perform various other actions. Such trustable systems satisfy a number of expectations: they will not loose or alter information, they will not expose information to unintended third-parties, they will not fail to supply timely information, they will provide high quality and fast answers, and so on. Some institutions are completely computational, rely on algorithms and a computational infrastructure for their proper function, e.g., traditional security mechanisms for enforcing access control protocols.

Alternatively, some institutions have a human component: they require explicit human input for their function. For example, reputation management systems have to rely on feedback from users to produce high quality reputation values for people. Crowdsourcing systems produce high confidence answers to problems based almost completely on human input. In both cases, the human input is solicited as part of a computational backbone that incorporates many design decisions, e.g., how participants should be recruited, how their answers should be combined and when answers should be disregarded. Recommendation systems are another example of institutions dependent on human input obtained from the digital footprint of its users. In this case, the human input is implicit. There are also recommendation systems based on explicit recommendations that are aggregated over the network. Institutions that rely heavily on the quality of human input need to take into consideration the possible impact of social and cognitive factors in their computation: human cognition, social ties, incentives for the use of systems and so on.

The same division between trusting actions and trusting information exists in the design of different systems. Institutions designed to enable economic and social activities tend to target trust for actions. In contrast, institutions designed to enable information exchange or education target trust for information. However, these two concepts remain closely related. Often, trust contexts are complex and involve

S. Adali, *Modeling Trust Context in Networks*, SpringerBriefs in Computer Science, DOI 10.1007/978-1-4614-7031-1_4, © The Author(s) 2013

many different constructs. For example, Wikipedia is an institution designed to create correct, comprehensive and authoritative information on a large number of topics. Wikipedia itself is a complex institution. It incorporates many computational elements that continuously monitor content, highlight suspicious activity and correct style related programs. There is a strong organizational component to Wikipedia as well that dictates how editors are elected and what their editorial powers are.

These complex institutions reflect today's reality: systems and people are networked: human and machine computation are intertwined in many different ways. It is possible for systems to make use of people to solve problems and for people to rely on machines to help reduce complexity of their every lives. Some institutions also "compute trust", meaning that they algorithmically assess how much another entity should be trusted. We will describe the various contexts implied by such computations in this chapter as we explore the issue of trust in this complex networked world.

4.1   Trustable Systems and Entities

The increasing diffusion of the Internet into daily life has led to the development of many different systems and entities, i.e., institutions, that are crucial to trust. A trustable institution is one that enables people to perform tasks that require trust. These tasks are evolving every day as more people become online and find new applications. The institutions that people rely on are always in flux, but their importance is undeniable [46]. People and businesses use computer systems to carry out transactions, communicate and store vital information. Automated systems monitor how our car runs, regulate the temperature in buildings, and manage energy fluctuations in the electric grid. Automated agents carry out complex financial transactions and give us advice on where to have lunch. We will treat these systems as institutional support for online trust.

4.1.1   System and Data Security

One of the earliest uses of the term trust is in system security. System security spans concepts from hardware and software to communications. A secure system is trustable. It correctly identifies the people accessing the system and only allows authorized people to use it. Data security ensures that people have access only to the information that they are allowed to see. No unauthorized person can access or change data. The access rights are not ambiguous or conflicting. Systems are capable of verifying that data has arrived from a specific source and was not modified along the way. Systems do not lose data. Systems ensure security even in the presence of adversaries who are trying to undermine their correct operation. A secure system is used by people for the purpose it is designed for: storing and sending information, or performing crucial infrastructure functions. Hence, such systems can be relied on by a person or another automated agent for these functions. Security alone may refer to different goals that require trust, from transmitting and storing information to solving problems. In the taxonomy offered by Grandison et al. [31], the closest term to this type of trust construct is "infrastructure trust". It refers to one's trust that a system will work properly. Security plays a major role in this problem. Often, the capability of the systems to carry out their function is not a concern in security, just the fact that they perform their function as intended. In the canonical taxonomy, this corresponds to integrity of systems. We discuss this distinction shortly.

Security is complicated further by considerations of privacy and ownership of data. Information providers may ensure security (to some degree), but may choose to mine the personal data of their users for business purposes or sell it to third parties. In this case, data security is still compromised if the usage violates the users' intent to keep their data private. When systems or data are controlled by entities other than the trustor, it is also important to consider whether these entities can be trusted to keep data secure. In the networked world, we increasingly use systems that are controlled by entities other than ourselves. For example, more and more data is now stored in "the cloud". As a result, understanding whether systems are trustable ultimately involves non-computational factors like the terms of use as well as computational ones.

Computing infrastructure also includes the people who use it. Actions of people may end up harming a system and compromising its security. For example, there are still people who use "password" as their password or simply keep default passwords unchanged. It can be much easier to get people to give up sensitive information than to break into secure systems to extract this information. People are generally unaware of consequences of their actions when it comes to computer security [75]. How can we measure how "secure" or "trustable" a system is by taking into account the human component? For example, the push for stronger passwords makes it even harder for people to remember them. This may lead users to employ simple heuristics for constructing passwords which in turn make systems even more vulnerable.

One of the approaches suggested to help human users enforce security is to introduce an appropriate a mental model [11], such as an analogy to public health. When the majority of a population is vaccinated against a disease, the whole public is safe similar to the notion of herd immunity. Hence, the actions required to keep a system secure, like installing necessary patches and virus software contributes to the security of the whole infrastructure. Such a mental model may help users to justify why certain actions are beneficial and modify their behavior. Another analogy is market-based. Secure systems contribute to a public good, and vulnerable machines pose a potential financial loss. This approach is very similar to some of the approaches used to compute trust. Other methods involve employing large groups of people playing online games to identify threats, improving the response time and accuracy of such methods by relying on high volume of data provided by the players [61]. Such an approach trusts people to help enhance security methods.

To summarize, security and privacy are important components of designing trustable systems. Security spans many different trust goals from secure communication to secure data storage. While the underlying methodology for ensuring security is usually the main topic of study in computer science research, the human input in such systems cannot be ignored. Computers must trust people to enforce and enhance security. It is not yet clear whether an analytic model exists to quantify security, i.e., trustability, when we mix algorithmic methods with systems that rely on the emergent properties of the underlying design such as those in game based approaches [61].

4.1.2   Identity

An important component of security is authentication: being able to correctly identify a person. Nissenbaum [59] discusses three barriers to establishing trust with another person in an online setting. The first is disembodiment which separates one from others in time and space, due to infrequent face-to-face interactions. This also means that one's identity is not tied to her physical presence. The second barrier is the new and sometimes inscrutable social contexts enabled by online applications. The roles people play in these applications do not have a clear social meaning. For example, suppose a person has been intimate with a person other than her spouse in an online game. Does this count as cheating? These two barriers are tied to the problem of identifying a person in an online setting, which is the third barrier. In online settings, identity is fluid. A person can create multiple identities easily and take on different social personas in each. If he misbehaves in one identity, he can quickly create a new one. This makes it hard to impose sanctions on users and obtain crucial information about their trustworthiness. This is a major problem for systems that require reliable reputation management mechanisms. In essence, more accurately someone can be identified, the harder it is for him to misbehave. On the other hand, there are many instances where being able to remain anonymous is crucial. For example, social activists fighting against oppressive regimes and drug cartels might only be able to make an impact if they can stay anonymous. Otherwise, they risk being killed or subjected to cruel treatment [57]. Hence, the goals of identity management systems very much depend on the underlying application.

Online communities provide a good case study in the practice of identity management. Cryptography ensures that content encoded with a specific private key is signed by a specific person, but it does not identify who the owner is. In fact, it does not even ensure that the owner of this private key kept it "secret". Thus, the technology does not necessarily solve the problem of identity. To address this issue, various cryptography algorithms allow people to digitally sign each other's public keys. This practice creates a web of endorsements between individuals, sometimes referred to as the "Web of Trust". There is no limit to how many people can sign a key; the more endorsement there is for a key, the more trustworthy is its owner. The common practice is to conduct a "key signing" meeting within a specific community in which members decide on the rules for identifying each other through external means and counting votes. For example, open source communities rely on being able to identify people who contribute code to ensure the integrity of their project. The importance of the Web of Trust in the creation of Debian Linux is discussed in [60].

4.1.3 System Capability and Reliance on Automation

There is a great deal of research concentrated on making automated systems or intelligent agents trustable by humans [48]. We discussed this issue to some degree in Sect. 3.2.3. In computer science literature, the term delegation is sometimes used to describe situations in which a person relies on a computer to carry out an action on her behalf [31, 41] (Fig. 4.1). Relying on an automated system to place bids on eBay is an example of delegation. Another term used in this context is service provision, in which software agents perform an action. A system that provides the best recommendations or an email service that blocks junk mail are examples of service provision. The main concern in using such services is that they perform the function that they are designed to do (integrity) and that they perform it well (capability). These two aspects closely resemble the aspects we have discussed in trust belief with respect to people. System integrity spans multiple constructs, from security to overall system reliability. For example, a computer infected with a virus no longer has integrity. Its behavior is no longer predictable. We will examine integrity in more detail in the following sections.

Making systems more capable while at the same time making sure people do not overestimate their capabilities is a crucial component of making these systems trustable and trusted. For example, one does not want an automation's input to overwrite a person's common sense. People who rely on automated systems and

Fig. 4.1 Trust in automation

services should have an opportunity to observe their function and to develop trust beliefs with respect to such systems [48]. As a system becomes trusted, people may monitor it less frequently [56], hence reducing the cognitive load necessary to continuously evaluate its functionality. As a result, similar to the evaluation of capability of other individuals, positive evidence may start to carry larger weight. Trust for such systems may continue to grow even if occasional faults occur. However, if the overall reliability of the system declines, the trust will also decline over time. As a result, if sporadic faults can have a major impacts on the system's functionality, the design must take into consideration that these faults may not be correctly perceived by its user.

There is ongoing discussion regarding whether machines will ever be perceived as having positive intentions towards their users [34]. People often attribute social features to the systems they use, by considering them to be friendly and competent [58]. However, person-machine relationships are perceived differently than person-person relationships according to brain activation patterns. Hence, it is not clear to which degree an analogy with person to person trust relationships can be drawn when designing trustable systems.

Furthermore, systems incorporate the intentions of those who built them. The trust for different entities plays a role in judging the benevolence of their products. For example, Alice learns that her phone is recording all her activities and sending them to the device manufacturer. The system still has integrity, because it turns out that this was part of its design. However, Alice now knows that the system may expose very sensitive information about her to third parties and doubts about how benevolent the design is. Overall, there is a component of benevolence in system design that cannot be disregarded.

4.1.4 Reputation

Reputation is one of the most widely studied trust concepts. Reputation in social networks corresponds to what is generally said or believed about a person's character or standing. A person's reputation is public, determined by the common opinion of others in her social group. It indicates an expectation of adherence to the common norms of behavior in the given social group. One's actions, opinions of others, and recommendations in the group all contribute to one's reputation. In many open systems like e-commerce sites, people interact with others that they do not know beforehand. When one does not have firsthand knowledge about a person, his reputation can serve as a basis for trust. This is only possible if one's reputation will be damaged if he misbehaves. Reputation is relatively straightforward in face to face networks, but becomes more challenging in online systems where people can create new identities easily. If a person cheats in one transaction and ruins the reputation of an identity, he can easily create another one. Reputation management systems aim to improve this situation by providing useful information about trustees that can be used to form beliefs about their trustworthiness.

Kollack [46] discusses the main properties that reputation management systems should have to be effective tools for informing others of users' trustworthiness. First, the cost of providing data to impact a trustee's reputation should be low, hence allowing the collection of large volumes of data. Second, there should be many alternative trustees, hence reducing the dependence on any single trustee for a specific good or service. Third, the cost of impersonating a trustee and gaining good reputation should be high. This means that good identity management systems are needed for both trustors and trustees. Additional mechanisms are needed to make sure malicious agents cannot alter a good seller's reputation. Finally, the reputation method should itself be trustworthy, ensuring that it is unbiased and secure.

Reputation and trust management for reputation have been topics of intense study in the computing literature [35,40,41,42] and in information sciences [6,17,18,19]. Reputation management methods are often designed for online e-commerce sites that allow buyers and sellers to interact with each other. The main goal is to provide buyers accurate information about the sellers. These systems rely on feedback from buyers about the performance of the sellers, both positive and negative. This information is then aggregated and presented to the buyers as an estimate of the sellers' trustworthiness. Many design decisions impact the computation of reputation: how often buyers are allowed to evaluate sellers, how information is presented to buyers to seek their feedback, how information is aggregated, whether past information can be forgotten or changed, whether the reputation management system can plant fake ratings, and how reputation information is presented to the buyers. Reputation systems may seek information about specific transactions and aggregate these to compute reputation. Some reputation systems also allow users to directly rate each other for trustworthiness and use this to compute reputations. In this case, the trustworthiness of the rater can be taken into consideration when considering her input.

In e-commerce sites like eBay, trustors are not typically concerned with assessing trustees' ability; the transaction itself is usually not hard to accomplish. However, the integrity of the trustee is in question. Do they represent the product that they are selling truthfully? Will they ship the item quickly? Most reputation systems designed in this context are based on sanctions. When a seller behaves badly, this must have a serious impact in his reputation. In fact, a theoretical result shows that aggregating the past history of a trustee does not improve the effectiveness of the reputation system from an economic point of view [17]. This is similar to how people evaluate the "trustworthiness" and "friendliness" of other people: negative information is considered more diagnostic. It is irrelevant if the person behaved well many times; if they betray trust once, they are not trustworthy.

A second type of reputation system is designed to judge the quality of the service provided by a trustee. This is especially important for online sites that aim to promote themselves as trustworthy entities to shop from: do they provide high quality products that last a long time? Are they great at packing the items they ship? Reputation mechanisms designed to judge the capability of trustees are based on signaling [18,19]. In such cases, the more information there is about a specific item of interest, the more informed the user will feel. This is the reason that most online sellers incorporate a forum where users can freely rate and review the products. As with judgments of capability in Sect. 3.2, more information adds more value. In fact, researchers have investigated whether it is beneficial to plant fake product reviews and remove bad user reviews to inflate the site's reputation artificially. The theoretical results are interesting: sellers will optimize their benefits if all the reputation systems contain only true feedback [18]. However, since some sites will inevitably manipulate their online forums, a site that does not follow suit will suffer. However, signaling can also help in judging trustworthiness of e-commerce sites: sites that have online forums are perceived to have more transparency and are considered more trustworthy compared to sites that do not support such forums.

A trustworthy reputation system should be robust which means that it should be hard to manipulate a person's reputation via an attack from a small number of individuals. Josang and Golbeck discuss types of possible attacks on reputation systems [39]. Among these are attacks in which a person achieves good reputation and uses it to impact someone else's reputation (playbook), a group of individuals give bad marks to a single seller to impact her reputation (collusion), or a bad seller leaves the system and enters under a new identity (re-entry). A good reputation system must reduce the impact of these type of attacks as much as possible.

In addition to economic transactions between peers mediated by a third-party system, reputation methods have been used in purely peer to peer systems [1,76,78] that facilitate interaction between peers distributed over a network (e.g., BitTorrent). In such systems, there is no central authority that contains all the relevant trust information about the participants. The computing platform provides the capability to communicate with peers, perform tasks (e.g., file sharing), and transmit information about the success of operations and possible trust evaluations. The users compute trust for their peers based on the information available to them. As a result, the computed trust may differ from peer to peer. This subjective value provides a different measurement than reputation, which is a global value. In both cases, trust values are computed to protect the peers from harm by making sure that attacks cannot result in unwarranted trust or reputation values.

Overall, reputation is an institutional mechanism. A trustor visiting a site will rely on its reputation mechanism to decide to which degree a trustee is trustworthy (unless she has previous experience with the trustee). Many sites have become successful due to the reliability of their specific reputation mechanisms, such as Amazon and Ebay. Reputation mechanisms have also been employed in sites for sharing information, e.g., Slashdot, in which a user with good reputation is expected to post high quality and correct information.

4.1.5   Ranking Web Pages

One of the earliest uses of trust, even though it was not explicitly called such, was in the ranking of web pages in response to a query. Before the now famous-link analysis algorithms like PageRank [9] became common-place, the information retrieval literature concentrated mostly on optimizing performance for relevance: finding the most relevant answer for a given keyword query. This was natural when the search was among sources of equal quality. However, this is not the case for the Web. As an open publishing medium, Web contains much redundant information with various degrees of quality. As a result, there are potentially (too) many web pages that are relevant to a specific query. For a search engine to be useful, it must rank pages that are considered to be correct, authoritative, and up to date higher than the rest. Hence, search engines determine rank by trustability of information as well as relevance. The problem is then developing methods to infer the trustability of information on the Web.

Today's search engines use many different signals, from the popularity of a page in terms of number of clicks to its update frequency. Link analysis algorithms are also widely used, treating a hyperlink between two pages as a vote of confidence from the source page to the destination page. Studies show that people treat these links as endorsements of the trustworthiness of destination sites [71]. Link analysis algorithms borrow from social networking literature, in which such votes can be used to understand the network location of a person: central locations tend to imply more important people. Using this analogy, algorithms like PageRank [9] and Hits [45] compute a score for each page, which can be considered an estimate of its importance or authority. The success of PageRank is one of the main reasons for the early success of Google. Many variations of these algorithms have been introduced, and ranking algorithms have become much more sophisticated over time.

As Web grows larger and is used by an ever increasing group of people, these earlier approaches for computing trust have become insufficient [2]. Link analysis algorithms assume that sites link to other sites because there is a relevant or important piece of information on those sites. The network constructed in this way has an emergent property that can be captured by various notions of centrality. In the early years, this assumption was correct. The Web was a natural extension of the interests and views of the site creators. The wisdom of crowds meant that if a site was high-quality, it would be linked by many others and algorithms like PageRank worked perfectly.

In today's Web, having a site that is highly ranked by search engines and especially Google has significant social and financial implications. Due to the increasing number of content publishers, the proportion of high quality sites to others for a specific topic is getting increasingly smaller [7,24]. Sites are competing for the limited attention of information consumers. In fact, as early as in 2,000, studies showed that 80 % of site visits are to just 0.5 % of Web sites despite the availability of diverse sources of information [74]. As a result, site publishers started to add links to boost their own ranking using link farms [32] and other web optimization tools. This meant that the original meaning of a link was no longer true: links could also be created to increase prominence of a site regardless of its content. The effectiveness of link analysis algorithms has decreased as links have become less correlated with the quality of content.

To address this issue, a new generation of link aggregation algorithms have been developed. These new methods first find trustworthy sites, either previously given to the algorithm or constructed from statistics that are hard to manipulate. Then, the algorithm assumes that the more trustworthy a site, the less likely it is to link to a spam site [33].

The ranking of web pages is another type of reputation computation that is partially based on link analysis algorithms. The rank computation assigns a score of importance to each page, with the implication that higher-ranked pages are likely to be more trustworthy. This is combined with methods that determine relevance. Link analysis methods use a network that is shaped both by human activity (e.g., site creation and linking to other sites) as well as automated systems (e.g., link farms and web site creation tools). These algorithms have to consider that there are adversaries in the system that are not benevolent and correctly identify them.

However, web ranking is not identical to traditional reputation management. Due to the highly redundant nature of the Web, it is not important to rank all the pages correctly, only those returned at the top. Furthermore, in reputation management systems, there is usually no underlying network of relationships, which is crucial for link analysis methods. Finally, it is still not clear how to distinguish a good link from a bad link, e.g., a positive endorsement vs. a link given to criticize another site. Adding semantics to links has been proposed as a solution, in which a link may contain a special "nofollow" tag. This is now commonly used by wikis and discussion groups. Investigating how these links could be processed with traditional network analysis methods is a topic of research [49].

Economic and political competition will continue to encourage individuals to manipulate page rankings to their benefit through new means. Hence, trust for ranking algorithms depends on the degree to which they can be manipulated by the agendas of self-interested actors [20].

4.1.6 Crowdsourced Information

Many information services benefit from the wisdom of crowds. Due to the sheer volume of information and interactions on the Internet, systems can make the assumption that if a piece of information is reliable, then a lot of people will endorse it. This is incorporated into link analysis algorithms, as we have seen in the previous section. Crowdsourcing methods improve the trustworthiness of information by explicitly seeking a large amount of independent human input for a problem [21,69]. These methods are designed to seek input from individuals who do not have a personal stake in the final answer, avoiding the problems associated with selfish agents. For example, the Amazon Turk system was originally developed to cheaply conduct tasks that are hard for a computer to perform but effortless for people. It allows individuals to be paid small sums for performing simple tasks. Today, Amazon Turk is used widely for diverse purposes, from conducting user studies for understanding user perceptions towards various factors [43] to data curation for finding duplicate and incorrect information [50].

Another phenomenon common in China is called Human Flesh Search [72] in which a very large number of individuals collaborate online to solve a specific problem. In Amazon Turk each individual is asked to answer a simple question. In contrast, in human flesh search, individuals actively seek and disambiguate information to help solve a more complex problem. Many other examples of such collaborations exist, in which users analyze images to help astronomers identify galaxies or collaborate in scavenger hunts [62].

When judging trust for information computed using such methods, several important factors need to be considered, such as the intent and competence of the participants, the size of the input set and the problem design. Furthermore, various factors such as demographics can be used to judge to which degree the input from different participants can be considered independent and representative.

4.1.7 Online Organizations: Wikipedia and Open Source Software

In more complicated examples of crowdsourcing, participants collaborate on complex tasks over the course of creating a common product. To ensure that the product is reliable (i.e., trustable or credible), the participants often create a governance structure with rules that describe how content can be modified and defines user roles. Hence, online collaborations eventually evolve into an organizational structure.

The most well-known example is Wikipedia, an online ever-changing encyclopedia created with the contributions of volunteers that has been proven to be as credible as many established encyclopedias [28]. Research shows that as Wikipedia has grown and become an established institution for trustworthy content, more and more of the interaction between content providers is dedicated to conflict resolution [44]. To overcome this problem, Wikipedia instituted a complex set of rules for reviewing content and reaching a consensus [10]. The human effort is complemented with software agents that find and flag vandalism, and correct HTML coding errors to maintain a uniform and trustworthy presentation. However, studies show that Wikipedia content still shows biases that reflect the biases of the community of volunteers such as the representation of topics of interest to them with longer and more detailed articles [38]. Similarly, the quality of articles on topics of little interest to the community is likely to be lower. Trust in Wikipedia is an ongoing effort, studied from many perspectives [65].

Another area in which trust is studied is the development of open-source software by collaborations of individuals who do not know each other. Increasingly, open-source projects obtain investments from equity firms and developed projects are incorporated into commercial applications [68]. The importance of Web of Trust for identifying the participants of a project was discussed in Sect. 4.1.2. Individuals also require methods to decide how to incorporate changes made by different contributors into the main project. Different organizational structures have been adopted for these virtual organizations [26, 37].

In such systems, software is not simply a product of developers that provide code. The support of the greater online community is also crucial. The user community uses the software, reports bugs and contributes patches. As the user community grows larger, it becomes more likely that software is well-tested and trusted. Furthermore, the user community provides online tutorials and code examples that further encourage others to use the system. Hence, an open-source software and any system built on it is trusted to be stable and free of bugs if the community that supports it is deemed healthy.

4.2 Trust as a Belief

In the previous section, we reviewed several online institutions related to trust. In this section, we review literature that treats trust as a belief that the trustor has about the trustee. There are a number of threads of literature in this field. The first thread builds on the trust literature in social and cognitive trust to assess who trusts whom in online social networks. The aim of this type of work is to build new information services by making use of this information. To accomplish this, systems try to estimate how much or whether one person trusts another person. In some cases, the person may distrust another. This is a type of link prediction [47]. The hope is then more trustworthy information or services can be built based on these trust relationships.

The second thread involves building intelligent agents that can trust each other based on a theoretical conceptualization of trust. These computational agents evaluate each other's trustworthiness based on various characteristics of the trustees' behavior and adjust their actions accordingly. The hope is that with an accurate assessment of trust, the agents can expose themselves to as little risk as possible while utilizing available resources optimally. While the trust construct used in this work is often inspired by social and cognitive constructs, it is more idealized. The system performance that the agents are optimizing is used to define the desirable properties of trust computation. We have discussed some of this type of computation in Sect. 4.1.4 and we will discuss other examples in Sect. 4.2.2.

4.2.1 Social Trust

Many online networking sites make it possible for people to communicate directly with friends or acquaintances. In these sites, people can choose to remain anonymous or expose their true identity. Popular sites like facebook, Twitter, and reddit are designed mostly to share information with others. Other sites are used for sharing photos (flickr), location (foursquare), and videos (YouTube). Ultimately, researchers want to understand to which degree a site is used to make social connections with others and form communities. This is only possible if people are interacting with each other directly. The more likely it is that people will meet again, the more likely it is that they will form social connections, if such connections do not already exist. For example, reddit has many subforums; some are based on a topic and some are based on a community, like a university or a town. The smaller the community, the more likely that people will know or get to know each other.

In some cases, online social networks are a continuation of existing social relationships in the physical world. They simply allow people who know each other to communicate. In other cases, they allow new relationships to form under real or invented identities. For example, in online games, sometimes people interact with characters they only know within the game context. Generally, online social networks form around a shared interest, background, point of view or story. Trust is crucial in some of these sites. They allow people to take actions that are not otherwise possible (e.g., coordinating massive public demonstrations) and share private information (e.g., helping people share personal health stories and give advice to each other anonymously in online forums). Sites like CouchSurfing allow people to stay in each other's houses when they are traveling. People give micro-loans to those who need them via sites like Kiva. People collaborate on software development on sites like Advogato and engage each other in research discussions on ResearchGate. Entrepreneurs test the demand for new products by Kickstarter campaigns. All these actions require trust.

A site's design may establish specific reputation mechanisms to help its users. Some sites allow people to provide explicit trust rankings of each other, which are then aggregated to a reputation rating. Alternatively, the design may provide an environment in which people can establish their own rules and behavioral norms. These norms are enforced by non-verbal [77] or verbal cues. For example, the well-publicized reddit etiquettes or reddiquettes are an example of a verbal norm, which is enforced by messages by others. Free speech is very strongly supported in reddit, so votes for posts generally imply that the post is relevant to a subreddit. This is enforced by other redditors who criticize inappropriate behavior in their comments, e.g., downvoting someone because they do not like a post is not tolerated. If this does not work, moderator actions are taken.

Research is still ongoing on the topic of whether the Internet provides completely new norms of behavior and social organizations, or it extends existing patterns in an incremental way [20]. One of the fertile areas of study is how people use these sites to form trust relationships and improve credibility of information, and to verify the validity of rumors and stop the spread of incorrect information. We will study trust in information in Sect. 4.3. Tend et al. [4] study the trust ratings in different social media sites. They find that the ratings of people for each other on social media sites are generally very positive if it is made public who voted how for whom. However, people are willing to give more candid ratings in private. Hence, any trust algorithm has to take into account the social and community context for a rating.

The second area of study is to determine who trusts whom and how the trust can be quantified based on existing social interactions and explicit ratings [29]. This concept is different than reputation which computes how much people should trust a specific person. The type of trust algorithm discussed here addresses how likely people are to trust each other. Trust is not necessarily a symmetric construct; Alice may trust Bob but Bob may not trust Alice. Most algorithms also discuss when it is possible to infer transitivity: when Alice trusts Bob and Bob trusts Charlie, is it the case that Alice trusts Charlie as well? From a computational perspective, necessary and sufficient conditions for transitivity are examined in [5]. However, in small friendship circles, transivity can be explained easily. If Alice is friends with Bob and Bob is friends with Charlie, it is likely that Alice, Bob and Charlie all hang out together and are friends. As a result, they are friends with each other based on the transitive closure of social relations. This type of transitivity is used frequently in community detection algorithms. A community is generally characterized as a (small) group of individuals that are more tightly connected to each other than to the outside world. Note that transitivity in this case describes the component of trust that we characterized as trustworthiness, warmth or friendliness. It does not capture competence which is not likely to be transitive. However, there might be external reasons that would imply transitivity in competence. For example, Alice, Bob and Charlie may all know each other from a prestigious college and expect that they have certain competencies as a result.

Some work aims to understand which social behavior is a more likely indicator of a friendship and which social behavior is a good indicator that a person is (also) trusted for their competence [3]. Other work is based on the direct evaluations of trust [22]. Using these constructs and assumptions, trust algorithms find a quantitative trust value for different pairs of individuals. This type of trust computation is especially useful for developing customized services for individuals. For example, the well-known social phenomena of homophily implies that Alice's friends tend to share's Alice's interests [54]. In fact, Alice's friends tend to do similar things as Alice [15] due to the social influence friends have on each other. These findings are used for applications like targeted advertising and recommendation systems to help people find things of interest to them.

4.2.2   Trusting Agents

Trust is also used in the design of agent-based systems in which each agent evaluates how much it trusts the other agents based on their behavior. The term "Semantic Web" was coined by Berners-Lee, Hendler and Lassila [8] who imagined a set of standards that allowed for devices and applications to communicate with each other at a semantic level. Trust is a foundational element of this vision, allowing agents to decide when to trust each other. Policies must be designed to describe how agents can broker trust relationships by verifying and requesting various types of tokens, assuming the proper authentications methods are already in place.

The trust models of intelligent agents are often inspired by cognitive trust. Agents have internal beliefs and act on them. They make recommendations about who can be trusted and who should be distrusted. Sometimes there are central trusted authorities, and sometimes trust computation is distributed to each agent. Sometimes the agents emulate social and cognitive trust, but take care not to become vulnerable because of it. Issues of concern in the design of these agents range from assessing the intent of other nodes, whether they are selfish or not, how their propensity to trust impacts their trust beliefs, how they incorporate evidence about trust into their current beliefs [73], whether and how they forget about past evidence [51,52,78] and so on. An important consideration is when the computed value can be considered a measure of trust, but not a probabilistic estimate of reliability [23]. Another concern is making sure that computed trust value is useful for the agent's function, which is not necessarily a conscious concern in the cognitive notion of trust.

The term trust is routinely used in computer networking to refer to this type of measures computed by agents. An agent situated at a computational node observes the success and failure of packets routed through other nodes. It sends recommendations about other nodes in the network to help them form trust impressions about their neighbors [14, 30]. These methods incorporate algorithms to establish how much the trustor should trust the trustee (trust computation and update), which trust information should be sent to other nodes (recommendations) and how to inform other nodes when a node should no longer be trusted (trust revocation). These actions taken together constitute a trust management scheme. Trust computation enhances the existing routing methods by routing through trusted peers.

4.3   Trust in Information

Trust in information has been studied extensively on the Internet. The exchange of information is one of the primary uses of the Internet. Early research in this area investigated the signals users rely on to judge the credibility of content found online. We discussed research in this area in detail in Sect. 3.3. In particular, the look and feel of a site serves an important role in the formation of quick judgments about whether the site is professional and contains current information. Various seals of approval provided by outside institutions, help enforce this view [53]. The user's expertise in the search area and the sites' relevance to the topic are among the many factors that determine a user's trust based on the site's content [27]. The reputation of the sources also contribute to the judgments for trust in content. A site's reputation can be based on its ranking in search engines, links from other sites, or other recommendations. However, this information is replaced by the user's own judgment as she gains experience with the site [25] (Fig. 4.2).

Analysis of a site's content is costly in terms of cognitive resources, and is likely to replaced by heuristics based on secondary cues like appearance [36]. In some instances, the individual lacks either the desire or the ability to engage in systematic processing of content. However, in other cases, the individual is engaged in a purposeful effort to understand a specific topic by building a mental model of what information is available [63]. A quick review of available sites is used to judge

Fig. 4.2 Trust in information

the credibility of the sources and information they provide [67]. Certain information can be considered more credible because it agrees with the majority of sites on this topic (unless of course they all appear to be copies of the same page). Over time, a user may rely on her judgment about the content more than the credibility of the source, combining facts from different sources when necessary to form an answer to a query. Research in this area shows that when information credibility is concerned, it is important to understand the trust for the sources as well as the trustor's mental model. The relationship between the two co-evolves continuously with the help of many different types of cues.

People also incorporate social signals to judge information credibility. This especially true in situations where information travels very quickly and there is limited opportunity to verify its validity by relying on more reputable sources. Saavedraa et al. [66] study traders exchanging instant messages in an attempt to interpret and disambiguate information. In this case, the traders already trust each other and are not in direct competition. The authors show that people working together tend to synchronize their message exchange. The level of synchrony is a useful signal that shows that a consensus is being reached; the highest synchrony occurs when everyone agrees. Traders who could detect when the synchrony is starting to happen end up making the largest profits.

Social media is also used to spread misinformation and spam, sometimes with a political motive. For example, information often starts to get circulated quickly by a small group of individuals on the Internet, gets picked up by news agencies as fact, and then starts to become common wisdom due to its prominence on the Web [16,64]. In this case, if people can be fooled into sending misinformation, then those who trust them will further propagate it and increase its reach considerably in a short amount of time. Metaxas et al. [55] show that the support for real time content search contributes to rumors and misinformation becoming viral. Given that social media has been a crucial component of recent popular uprisings like those in Egypt and Tunisia [70], it is important to understand how people assess credibility in these sites. This is a growing area of interest, in which research tries to identify which social- and information- related signals are especially useful for understanding the expertise of the posters [12] and the credibility of the information [13]. There is still work to be done to understand the different roles people play in these sites, the level of risk involved in sharing information, and how these impact users' online behavior and information credibility.

References

1. K. Aberer, Z. Despotovic, Managing trust in a peer-2-peer information system, in *Proceedings of 10th International Conference on Information and Knowledge Management(CIKM01)*, Atlanta, pp. 310–317 (2001)
2. S. Adalı, T. Liu, M. Magdon-Ismail, An analysis of optimal link bombs. Theor. Comput. Sci. **437**, 1–20 (2012)
3. S. Adalı, M. Magdon-Ismail, F. Sisenda, Actions speak as loud as words: predicting relationships from social behavior data, in *Proceedings of the WWW Conference*, Lyon (2012)
4. L.A. Adamic, D. Lauterbach, C.Y. Teng, M.S. Ackermanm, Rating friends without making enemies, in *Proceedings of the AAAI Conference on Social Media and Weblogs (ICWSM 2011)*, Barcelona (2011)
5. R. Andersen, C. Borgs, J. Chayes, U. Feige, A. Flaxman, A. Kalai, V. Mirrokni, M. Tennenholtz, Trust-based recommendation systems: an axiomatic approach, in *Proceedings of WWW*, Beijing, pp. 199–208 (2008)
6. S. Ba, P.A. Pavlou, Evidence of the effect of trust building technology in electronic markets: price premiums and buyer behavior. MIS Q. **26**(3), 243–268 (2002)
7. F. Benevenuto, G. Magno, T. Rodrigues, V. Almeida, Detecting spammers on twitter, in *CEAS 2010 – Seventh annual Collaboration, Electronic messaging, Anti- Abuse and Spam Conference*, Redmond (2010)
8. T. Berners-Lee, J. Hendler, O. Lassila, The semantic web. Sci. Am. pp. 29–37 (2001)
9. S. Brin, L. Page, The anatomy of a large-scale hypertextual web search engine, in *Proceedings of the ACM WWW Conference*, Brisbane, Australia, pp. 107–117 (1998)
10. B. Butler, E. Joyce, J. Pike, Don't look now, but we've created a bureaucracy: the nature and roles of policies and rules in wikipedia, in *Proceedings of the twenty-sixth Annual SIGCHI Conference on Human Factors in Computing Systems, CHI '08*, (ACM, New York, 2008) Florence, Italy, pp. 1101–1110
11. L.J. Camp, Mental models of privacy and security. IEEE Technol. Soc. Mag. **28**(3), 1–10 (2009)
12. K. Canini, B. Suh, P. Pirolli, Finding credible information sources in social networks based on content and social structure, in *2011 IEEE International Conference on Privacy, Security, Risk, and Trust, and IEEE International Conference on Social Computing*, Boston, USA (2011)
13. C. Castillo, M. Mendoza, B. Poblete, Information credibility on twitter, in *Proceedings of the 20th International Conference on World Wide Web*, Hyderabad, pp. 675–684 (2011)
14. J.H. Cho, A. Swami, I.R. Chen, A survey on trust management for mobile ad hoc networks. IEEE Commun. Surv. Tutor. **13**(4), 562–583 (2010)
15. N.A. Christakis, J.H. Fowler, *Connected: The Surprising Power of Our Social Networks and How They Shape Our Lives.* (HarperCollins Publishers, New York, 2011)
16. O. Dabeer, P. Mehendale, A. Karnik, A. Saroop, Timing tweets to increase effectiveness of information campaigns, in *Proceedings of the AAAI Conference on Social Media and Weblogs (ICWSM 2011)*, Barcelona, Spain (2011)
17. C. Dellarocas, Reputation mechanism design in online trading environments with pure moral hazard. Inf. Syst. Res. **16**(2), 209–230 (2005)

18. C. Dellarocas, Strategic manipulation of internet opinion forums: implications for consumers and firms. Manage. Sci., **52**(10), 1577–1593 (2006)
19. C. Dellarocas, X.M. Zhang, N.F. Awad, Exploring the value of online product reviews in forecasting sales: the case of motion pictures. J. Interac. Mark. **21**(4), 23–45 (2007)
20. P. DiMaggio, E. Hargittai, W.R. Neuman, J.P. Robinson, Social implications of the internet. Annu. Rev. Sociol. **27**, 307–336 (2001)
21. A. Doan, R. Ramakrishnan, A.Y. Halevy, Crowdsourcing systems on the world-wide web. Commun. ACM **54**(4), 86–96 (2011)
22. T. DuBois, J. Golbeck, A. Srinavasan, Predicting trust and distrust in social networks, in *IEEE International Conference on Social Computing*, Boston, USA (2011)
23. R. Falcone, C. Castelfranchi, Trust dynamics: how trust is influenced by direct experiences and by trust itself, in *Proceedings of the Third International Joint Conference on Autonomous Agents and Multiagent Systems*, New York, USA, pp. 740–747 (2004)
24. D. Fetterly, M. Manasse, N. Najork, Spam, damn spam, and statistics: using statistical analysis to locate spam web pages, in *Proceedings of the International Workshop on the Web and Databases*, Paris, France, pp. 1–6 (2004)
25. K. Fullam, K. Barber, Dynamically learning sources of trust information: experience vs. reputation, in *Proceedings of the 6th International Joint Conference on Autonomous Agents and Multiagent Systems*, Honolulu, pp. 1–8 (2007)
26. M. Gallivan, Striking a balance between trust and control in a virtual organization: a content analysis of open source software case studies. Inf. Syst. J. **11**(4), 277–304 (2001)
27. Y. Gil, D. Artz, Towards content trust of web resources. Web Semant. **5**(4), 227–239 (2007)
28. J. Giles, Internet encyclopedias go head to head. Nature **438**(7070), 900–901 (2005)
29. J. Golbeck, Trust on the world wide web: a survey. Found. Trends Web Sci. **1**(2), 131–197 (2006)
30. K. Govindan, P. Mohapatra, Trust computations and trust dynamics in mobile adhoc networks: a survey. IEEE Commun. Surv. Tutor. **14**(2), 279–298 (2011)
31. T. Grandison, M. Sloman, A survey of trust in internet applications. IEEE Commun. Surv. Tutor. **3**(4), 2–16 (2000)
32. Z. Gyongyi, H. Garcia-Molina, Link spam alliances, in *Proceedings of the 31st International Conference on Very Large Data Bases*, Trondheim (2005)
33. Z. Gyongyi, H. Garcia-Molina, J. Pedersen, Combating web spam with trustrank, in *Proceedings of the 30th International Conference on Very Large Data Bases*, Toronto (2004)
34. P.A. Hancock, D.R. Billings, K.E. Schaefer, Can you trust your robot? Ergon. Des. **19**(3), 24–29 (2011)
35. C.J. Hazard, M.P. Singh, Intertemporal discount factors as a measure of trustworthiness in electronic commerce. IEEE Trans. Knowl. Data Eng **23**(5), 699-712 (2011)
36. B. Hilligoss, S.Y. Rieh, Developing a unifying framework of credibility assessment: construct, heuristics and interaction in context. Inf. Process. Manage. **44**, 1467–1484 (2008)
37. S. Hissam, D. Plakosh, C. Weinstock, Trust and vulnerability in open source software. IEEE Proc. Soft. **149**(1), 47–51 (2002)
38. T. Holloway, M. Bozicevic, K. Börner, Analyzing and visualizing the semantic coverage of wikipedia and its authors. Complexity **12**(3), 30–40 (2007)
39. A. Josang, J. Golbeck, Challenges for robust trust and reputation systems, in *Proceedings of the 5th International Workshop on Security and Trust Management (STM 2009)*, Saint Malo, France (2009)
40. A. Josang, R. Ismail, The beta reputation system, in *Proceedings of the 15th Bled Electronic Commerce Conference*, Bled, Slovenia (2002)
41. A. Josang, R. Ismail, C. Boyd, A survey of trust and reputation systems for online service provision. Decis. Support Syst. **43**(2), 618–644 (2007)
42. S. Kamvar, M. Schlosser, The eigentrust algorithm for reputation management in p2p networks. in *Proceedings of the 12th International Conference on World Wide Web*, Budapest, pp. 640–651 (2003)

43. A. Kittur, E.H. Chi, B. Suh, Crowdsourcing user studies with mechanical turk. in *CHI '08 Proceedings of the twenty-sixth annual SIGCHI conference on Human factors in computing systems*, Florence (2008)
44. A. Kittur, B. Suh, B.A. Pendleton, E.H. Chi, He says, she says: conflict and coordination in wikipedia, in *Proceedings of the SIGCHI Conference on Human Factors in Computing Systems, CHI '07*, San Jose (ACM, New York, 2007), pp. 453–462
45. R. Kleinberg, Authoritative sources in a hyperlinked environment. J. ACM **46**(5), 604–632 (1999)
46. P. Kollock, The production of trust in online markets, in *Advances in Group Processes (Vol. 16)*, ed. by E.J. Lawler, S.T.M. Macy, H. A. Walker (JAI, Greenwich, 1999)
47. U. Kuter, J. Golbeck, Sunny: a new algorithm for trust inference in social networks using probabilistic confidence models, in *AAAI*, Vancouver, pp. 1377–1382 (2007)
48. J.D. Lee, K.A. See, Trust in automation: designing for appropriate reliance. Hum. Factors **46**(1), 50–80 (2004)
49. J. Leskovec, D. Huttenlocher, J. Kleinberg, Predicting positive and negative links in online social networks, in *Proceedings of the 19th International Conference on World Wide Web*, Raleigh, pp. 641–650 (2010)
50. A. Marcus, E. Wu, D. Karger, S. Madden, R. Miller, Human-powered sorts and joins, in *Proceedings of Very Large Databases Conference (VLDB)*, Istanbul (2012)
51. S. Marsh, P. Briggs, Examining trust, regret and forgiveness as computational concepts, in *Computing with Social Trust*, ed. by J. Golbeck (Springer, London, 2009)
52. D.H. McKnight, N.L. Chervany, Trust and distrust definitions: one bite at a time, in *Trust in Cyber-Societies*, ed. by R. Falcone, M. Singh, Y.H. Tan. Lecture Notes in Artificial Intelligence, vol. 2246 (Springer, Berlin/New York, 2001), pp. 27–54
53. D.H. McKnight, C.J. Kacmar, Factors and effects of information credibility. In *ICEC*, University of Minnesota, Minneapolis, pp. 423–432 (2007)
54. M. McPherson, L. Smith-Lovin, J.M. Cook, Birds of a feather: homophily in social networks. Annu. Rev. Sociol. **27**(1), 415 (2001)
55. P.T. Metaxas, E. Mustafaraj, From obscurity to prominence in minutes: political speech and real-time search, in *Proceedings of Web Science Conference*, Raleigh (2010)
56. B. Muir, N. Moray, Trust in automation. part ii. experimental studies of trust and human intervention in a process control simulation. Ergonomics **39**(3), 429–460 (1996)
57. E. Mustafaraj, P. Metaxas, S. Finn, A. Monroy-Hernández, Hiding in plain sight: a tale of trust and mistrust inside a community of citizen reporters, in *Proceedings of the ICWSM Conference*, Dublin (2012)
58. C. Nass, Y. Moon, Machines and mindlessness: social responses to computers. J. Soc. Issues **56**(1), 81–103 (2000)
59. H. Nissenbaum, Will security enhance trust online, or supplant it? in *Trust and Distrust in Organizations*, ed. by R.M. Kramer, K.S. Cook. Russell Sage Foundation Series on Trust (Russell Sage Foundation, New York, 2004), pp. 155–188
60. S. O'Mahony, F. Ferraro, The emergence of governance in an open source community. Acad. Manage. J. **50**(5), 1079–1106 (2007)
61. B. Paulhamus, A. Ebaugh, C. Boylls, N. Bos, S. Hider, S. Gigure, Crowdsourced cyber defense: lessons from a large-scale, game-based approach to threat identification on a live network, in *Social Computing, Behavioral – Cultural Modeling and Prediction*, ed. by S. J. Yang, A.M. Greenberg, M. R. Endsley. Lecture Notes in Computer Science, vol. 7227 (Springer, Berlin/New York, 2012), pp. 35–42,
62. G. Pickard, I. Rahwan, W. Pan, M. Cebrian, R. Crane, A.S. Pentland Time critical social mobilization: the darpa network challenge winning strategy (2011), arXive.org 1008.3172v1
63. P. Pirolli, W.T. Fu, Snif-act: a model of information foraging on the world wide web, in *User Modeling 2003*, Johnstown, pp. 146 (2003)
64. J. Ratkiewicz, M.D. Conover, M. Meiss, B. Goncalves, A. Flammini, F.M. Menczer, Detecting and tracking political abuse in social media, in *Proceedings of the AAAI Conference on Social Media and Weblogs (ICWSM 2011)*, Barcelona (2011)

65. R. Rosenzweig, Can history be open source? wikipedia and the future of the past. J. Am. Hist. **93**(1), 117–146 (2006)
66. S. Saavedraa, K. Hagerty, B. Uzzi, Synchronicity, instant messaging, and performance among financial traders. *Proceedings of the National Academy of Sciences (PNAS)*, pp. 1018462108v1–201018462 (2011)
67. E. Sillence, P. Briggs, P.R. Harris, L. Fishwick, How do patients evaluate and make use of online health information? Soc. Sci. Med. **64**, 1853–1862 (2007)
68. O. Siobhán, F. Ferraro, Managing the boundary of an 'open' project, in *IESE Research Papers* (2004)
69. M. Srivastava, T. Abdelzaher, B.K. Szymanski, Human-centric sensing. Phil. Trans. R. Soc. 370 ser. A **1958**, 176–197 (2012)
70. K. Starbird, L. Palen, (how) will the revolution be retweeted?: information diffusion and the 2011 egyptian uprising, in *Proceedings of the ACM 2012 conference on Computer Supported Cooperative Work*, Seattle, pp. 7–16 (2012)
71. K.J. Stewart, Trust transfer on the world wide web. Organiz. Sci. **14**(1), 5–17 (2003)
72. F.Y. Wang, D. Zeng, J.A. Hendler, Q. Zhang, Z. Feng, Y. Gao, H. Wang, G. Lai, A study of the human flesh search engine: crowd-powered expansion of online knowledge. IEEE Comput. **43**(8), 45–53 (2010)
73. Y. Wang, C.W. Hang, M.P. Singh A probabilistic approach for maintaining trust based on evidence. J. Artif. Intell. Res **40**, 221–267 (2011)
74. J. Waxman, *The Old 80/20 Rule Take One on the Jaw. Internet Trends Report 1999 REview* (Alexa Research, San Francisco, 2000)
75. R. West, The psychology of security. Commun. ACM **51**(4), 34–40 (2008)
76. L. Xiong, L. Liu, Building trust in decentralized peer-to-peer electronic communities, in *Fifth International Conference on Electronic Commerce Research (ICECR-5)* Montreal, Canada (2002)
77. N. Yee, J.N. Bailenson, M. Urbanek, F. Chang, D. Merget, The unbearable likeness of being digital: the persistence of nonverbal social norms in online virtual environments. CyberPsychol. Behav. **10**(1), 115–121 (2007)
78. B. Yu, M. Singh, K. Sycara, Developing trust in large-scale peer-to-peer systems, in *IEEE First Symposium on Multi-Agent Security and Survivability*, Drexel, pp. 1–10 (2004)

Chapter 5
Trust Context

In this chapter, we summarize the discussion in the previous chapters and refocus them in relation to the concept of trust context, especially in networks. As a complex high-order process, the study of trust requires a multi-disciplinary approach. Throughout this brief, we illustrated the role trust plays in many different types of networks from different points of view. On one hand, a computational system may trust the inputs provided by its users to provide services that form an institutional context. On the other hand, a person may trust social and computational institutions and other trustees to perform actions and to provide inputs that impact the functioning of different institutions. The use of the term "trust" in all these applications have some common elements.

To review our initial discussion of the term "trust", we note that trust evaluation involves a dependence relation: the trustor is dependent on a trustee (or trustees) to accomplish a certain task. The trustor is uncertain whether her trust is well-placed before making a decision, and her decision to trust makes her vulnerable. Under this general umbrella, we find many variations of how trust is modeled. Ultimately, it is these differences that define the trust context, the specific conditions under which trust evaluations differ. In this chapter, we take a broader view of trust context and describe some of the modeling challenges that networked applications need to address.

We outlined many different aspects of the trust context in the previous chapters. The first distinction we made was with respect to the trustor. If the trustor is a person, then we worry about human cognition and possible social contexts that she belongs to. For computational agents, the model of trust may depend on the underlying application. In many networked applications, this distinction is not so clear. People use computational tools to mediate their interactions, and computational agents rely on human input for their function. As a result, the more interesting problem to study is how these two come together as a network. What are the properties of this network? What types of dynamics can result in responses to changes in the network state? We discuss this in Sect. 5.1.

We also drew a distinction between trusting information and trusting actions. When trusting information, information has already been given and the trustor can

S. Adali, *Modeling Trust Context in Networks*, SpringerBriefs in Computer Science, DOI 10.1007/978-1-4614-7031-1_5, © The Author(s) 2013

choose to assess the credibility of the information herself in her evaluation of trust. When trusting another for actions, she has to decide whether or not to trust, before the action takes place. From a modeling perspective, this distinction can be easily captured by a dependence relation. The trustor is dependent on one or more trustees to varying degrees for her trust decision. One of the trustees can be herself to some degree, based on her familiarity with the problem domain. Modeling the complex dependence relations is a second important step in modeling trust. We will talk about dependence in more detail in Sect. 5.2.

We then outlined many different research threads that discuss how the various trust constructs are evaluated. Instead of looking at trust as a single type of belief, the trust context can outline the relevant beliefs that play a role in the evaluation of complex goals. In particular, these beliefs may impact each other and evolve differently. This is true even for computational agents that operate in complex environments, such as the co-robotics example we mentioned earlier. We discuss these issues in Sect. 5.3.

Finally, there are many additional environmental factors that can impact trust. We will review some of these in Sect. 5.4. We propose to view trust as a continuous process, in which the trustor's impression of the trustees evolves as new evidence becomes available. This is true at different time scales, from cognitive processing of signals of different complexity to changes in the underlying goals as a function of newly discovered evidence. The modeling challenge in this case is identifying the factors that can have a significant impact in the trust processing.

These four basic elements unwrap the notion of "trust context" across the large number of domains that we have overviewed. We find that these elements have been discussed in the literature to various degrees, but have not been brought together under a single umbrella. As socio-technological networks drive the development of applications with more complex trust contexts and new interdependencies, it is increasingly important to study trust in a holistic manner. Without models of trust that make explicit the assumptions underlying different trust computations drawing from many different disciplines and contexts, it is hard to achieve this task.

The following sections outline the main modeling problems that must be addressed for the study of trust in networks, discussed in decreasing order of generality, from the most general network-level concepts to the details of trust evaluation of individual subgoals. The different sections are part of a continuum. There are many open research problems in each area and that provide many interesting challenges to the study of trust in networks.

5.1   The Network View: Institutions Related to Trust

Throughout this brief, we discussed many institutions that take part in trust decisions. When talking about Alice's trust for Bob, it is equally important to consider Bob's trust for Alice. Alice and Bob come together in networks that provide many different institutions. Alice's actions impact Bob, and Bob's actions impact Alice. Furthermore, Alice and Bob impact many other components of the network, as they provide information and services that benefit others.

Often, our actions in the network are facilitated and constrained by our computational environment, the applications and the devices we use. These change how we construct our daily reality. It is possible to rely on anonymous others, without any social connection. We interact with many different computational agents and rely on them for many different tasks. The interfaces we use help us create a mental model of what their functions are and how reliable they are. We collaborate with others, in very large numbers, to create highly sophisticated artifacts (like Wikipedia and open source software). In all these examples, trust exists as a foundational element that describes the interdependence between the different components of the network. A modeling challenge is to understand the implications of these interdependencies. How do the connectivity in the network and other design decisions impact how trust evolves?

We have seen many different institutions related to trust, from cultural and organizational institutions to those that are based on algorithmic constructs. In information creation, we analyzed Wikipedia as a unique collection of organizational rules, participant activity and computational tools, all dependent on each other. The information in Wikipedia is constantly under attack, as many attempt to alter the content to serve specific interests. Understanding the vulnerabilities of a complex system like Wikipedia requires a network-based analysis. The organizational and computational elements impact the way the contributors can add and modify content, and what the readers will see. The contributors' interests, objectivity and level of involvement is a significant contributor to the reliability of content in user-created sites like Wikipedia.

Similarly, computational reputation methods are built on user input, i.e., people's evaluation of each other. The reliability of a reputation method is the main determinant of how much it can be trusted for a specific action. To a large degree, the output of the reputation method is dependent on the quality and quantity of the user input. A site with a large user base with many honest reviews is likely to have more reliable information about the reputation score of each individual. Furthermore, such sites tend to foster a community feel, which enhances the perception of the site's trustworthiness.

However, the actual reputation computation involves many other design decisions: which inputs to aggregate; forget or disregard; how much fake input to inject; how to aggregate the inputs and how to present the results. In some cases, this is done in the interest of increasing the volume of interactions and the associated user input, especially in cases where there is no initial basis for trust. These manipulations alter to which degree the reputation value is dependent on the underlying user input. However, the user input is also dependent on how an e-business site and sellers are viewed, how their feedback is sought, and to which degree they get attribution for their input. In short, reputation is a closed system dependent on trust and supports actions that require trust.

In other system-level dependencies, the health of computational infrastructures depend heavily on their users, and the use depends on their trustability. For example, communication channels are expected to transmit information without loss and distortion unless they are not operating properly or are compromised. Many security protocols work properly as long as the human operators behave as expected.

When modeling trust in complex environments, the system view is very important. Viewing trust as a passive belief that changes based on specific inputs can be very misleading if the inputs depend heavily on the beliefs as well. Understanding the system within which trust is a factor is a first step in defining the trust context. Depending on the underlying application, the pertinent aspects of the sytem-level details must be added to the trust model.

5.2 Complex Goals and Dependency Relations

Within the given network context, each trust decision may involve a complex goal with many subgoals. Often these subgoals correspond to different trustees and institutions that play a role in the decision. For example, when deciding on the purchase of an item from a seller in an online marketplace, many factors may be considered: the reputation of the seller and the marketplace based on possible prior experience, available reviews, recommendations by other customers and the trustworthiness. Similarly, when judging whether information can be trusted, factors considered may include the credibility of the information, the trustworthiness of the source, the reliability of the transmission medium, and the degree to which different social contacts have vetted the information.

In crowdsourcing methods, the main objective is often to design methods for soliciting user input to find solutions to hard problems. The reliability of the output is dependent on the user input as well as design of the problem and the incentives. In some cases, if a sufficient amount of input is collected, then the reliability of the output is not dependent on any individual user's reliability or ability as long as there is no underlying bias in the inputs.

When understanding the trust context, these subgoals and their importance, i.e., weight, in the trust decision have to be modeled. As discussed earlier, the weights may vary based on situational factors and some subgoals may be considered only under some specific conditions. Often, institutions provide generalized expectations for a trustee, which is particularly important when there is no firsthand information about him. For example, cultural norms may only play a role when there is no social context. The reviews about a seller are important when there is no transactional history with that particular seller. In that case, the reliability of the site hosting the reviews and the reviewers' trustworthiness play a role. If the number of reviews for an item is small, then each individual review's reliability is more important. After a large number of reviews are accumulated for a product, the average score and the number of reviews may be sufficient to assess the quality of the product.

Hence, even for the same problem, the dependence relation is not a static distribution of weights. The familiarity (or expertise) of the trustor in a specific domain is often a factor that has an impact on the weights. If the trustor has knowledge in a domain, then she can judge the credibility of information herself by relying on herself. When she is not capable of judging information herself, she may then rely more heavily on the reliability or expertise of the information sources for her trust decision. The corroboration of the information by many sources may play an important factor, especially to reduce the dependence on information sources that are not trusted. Hence, the trustor may seek out more information in domains where she is not an expert and does not have access to known and trusted sources. Also, the credibility of the information can be a significant factor in judging information trust. The credibility of information can be also based incorrectly on familiarity, instead of expertise. Information that is easy to understand and recall may be considered more credible. For example, if Alice is seeking an answer to a puzzle question, she may find an incorrect answer more credible than the correct answer if the former sounds more familiar than the latter.

These weights are also affected by the cognitive or other computational resources needed to compute the trust decision. Even though the trustor is capable of reviewing information, she may decide to rely on the source's trustworthiness in many cases, simply because it is easier to do so. This is especially true if the source is highly trusted. In that case, relying on the source does not carry any risk and hence there is little reason to judge the credibility of the information. Note that it is possible to find algorithmic equivalents of this type of approach that rely on specific trusted nodes for a computation, instead of aggregating over a network.

Hence, the second type of design decision in modeling trust involves determining the important subgoals for a trust decision and how they are combined. The trust context also defines how the weights of different subgoals change what conditions they depend on. Often these conditions correspond to how much information the trustor has for a specific subgoal. As a result, this is an appropriate place to model the uncertainty inherent in trust decisions as a function of the available information for evaluating trust.

5.3   Trust Constructs and Beliefs

Trust constructs associated with each individual subgoal build on the dependency relations. In the previous section, we talked about different subgoals and how the dependence on each subgoal may change contextually. This section concentrates on a single subgoal and how it is evaluated by further refining the above model.

When evaluating trust for another entity, we outlined two main dimensions that are common to many different threads of research: trustworthiness and competence. The trustworthiness construct describes the integrity, reliability, and positive intentions of the trustee. The competence construct describes the ability of the trustee to accomplish a task, to give correct information and so on. A specific trust subgoal may involve both constructs to some degree or may depend on a single one for the most part. The distinction between these constructs impacts trust models significantly. There are likely many differences in what signals are used to evaluate them, how they impact decisions and how firsthand evidence is incorporated into trust beliefs. Plus, these two beliefs are distinct: a trustee may be considered both trustworthy and competent, but it is also possible that the trustee is only considered either trustworthy or competent.

Trustworthiness is highly correlated with friendship, in-group characterizations, and having the same values. There is some evidence that negative evidence carries more weight. If our friend is acting trustworthy, this is not significant. Hence, the trustworthiness belief is not impacted very highly with positive evidence. However, if he does something wrong, the trustworthiness belief may change drastically. As with many cognitive constructs, strong inputs, i.e., very positive or negative experiences, are likely to make an impact on the trustworthiness beliefs. Trustworthiness beliefs have an affective component, e.g., relying on someone to come through for you, and are not dependent on a topic or a domain of expertise.

Faces play a major role in judging how trustworthy someone is, and are evaluated very quickly and with little effort. This, trustworthiness evaluations made through the assessment of faces are available before any other trust evaluation. Such first impressions can be eventually overwritten by information obtained through second-hand knowledge (stories, reviews, reputation ratings) and firsthand experiences (true social relations). However, research shows that first impressions have a significant impact and may impact how the new evidence for a trustee is viewed.

Having common values and shared intentionality is a major component of judging someone to be trustworthy. In fact, this is cited as the main reason that automated systems cannot be trusted in the same way as human beings. If the trustee is considered not to share the trustor's cultural values, then he is likely to be distrusted. This means that other factors do not matter. Furthermore, such a determination depends heavily on the level of risk. For a decision requiring a high level of risk, the trustor is likely to choose a trustee that she finds trustworthy, regardless of their competence.

An analogue of trustworthiness exists when evaluating information. The visual appeal and organization of a site offering information provides cues about how professional and reliable the information is. As with faces, these evaluations are made quickly and without much effort. Most people form a judgment about a site in a fraction of a second. This impacts which sites will be visited. If a site is not visited, it will not get a chance to be evaluated for trustworthiness and/or competence. This problem is similar to our discussion in Sect. 5.1.

There is also evidence that competence is a different type of belief. For example, positive evidence is considered more relevant for judging competence. The more evidence that demonstrates Bob's knowledge in a field, the more likely Alice will believe that he is an expert in that field. Alice may then be willing to forgive occasional errors by Bob. In fact, a well-studied problem in automation is to make sure people continue to pay attention to the operation of a system considered to be competent. Inability to monitor such systems appropriately may lead to major problems in high-risk situations. It is also likely that competence is specific to a topic. The generalizability of the belief concerning someone's competence depends on the different problem domains in which someone's ability is observed. Similar to trustworthiness, it is much more likely take notice of someone's competence if there is a strong evidence. If Bob is surrounded by many other competent candidates, Alice might not notice his abilities.

When judging the trust for a trustee, if sufficient information about his competence is not available, the trustor may use a heuristic and base her evaluation on his trustworthiness. The reverse is not necessarily true. In fact, the decision to rely on a trustee who is competent but not necessarily trustworthy may involve a rational evaluation of risks and potential benefits. A decision based on the trustworthiness of a trustee may be suboptimal from a rational perspective (as judged by utility theory). However, when benefits are viewed in the long term, one can find reasons to deal with a trustee who is trustworthy but not necessarily the most competent. Examples of such benefits are the ease of communication due to shared vocabulary and past experience with resolving conflicts, the possibility of benefitting from special favors and so on.

In short, trustworthiness and competence beliefs are not the same. They consider different inputs and evaluate evidence differently. In addition, the evaluation of one belief may impact the other in many different ways.

5.4 The Trust Evaluation Process

As is clear from the description in the previous sections, trust evaluation is not a single event, but a continuous process. On the smallest time scale, we consider how the processing of different signals relevant to different beliefs interacts with each other. For example, first impressions formed by the visual appearance of a site are available before reading the content. In some cases, a trustor may even stop processing of the content because she does not have enough cognitive resources or time, or feels she has enough information. The first impressions may significantly impact the trust evaluations formed by the later inputs.

We also discussed about many different interactions between the different signals in cognitive processing: paying attention to the highest signal, considering coherence among signals as a confirmation of their correctness, evaluating later signals differently due to the way earlier signals created expectations, and so on. This is studied in great detail in the polling literature [2] where questionnaires have to take into account question order, wording of questions, and priming factors that might impact the answers. People are known to make different decisions when faced with two different ways to phrase the same question. They are more likely to avoid something framed as a loss than pursue something framed as a gain [1].

This type of processing happens continuously at many time scales. In Chap. 1, Alice read several different online reviews, but the first review she read formed a baseline for her. As a result, she did not trust any review that contradicted the first review. Correctly or incorrectly, she had formed an opinion and was much more willing to trust information that confirmed her opinions. Overall, trust evaluations are continuously changed as different inputs become available, and new inputs are assessed as more processing time becomes available. Often, trust evaluation is viewed as a simple process, but this is far from the truth. As the trustor explores the information space, her knowledge of the problem domain may change considerably. This may impact her ability to process the credibility of new information she encounters.

Viewing trust evaluation as a continuous process instead of a single event brings new modeling considerations. By this, we do not mean the usual trust belief formation process. Typically, trust beliefs evolve slowly as new information about the trustee becomes available. These beliefs serve as a baseline in trust evaluation. At the same time, one can form impressions of the other person fairly quickly based on the available evidence. Impressions are situational and can change rapidly as the trustor gets new information about the trustee. When modeling these situational components, we must remember that the current trust impressions may be an input to the next phase of trust evaluation.

5.5   Conclusions

In this chapter, we outlined a framework for describing important components of trust context: those elements of trust that are situational and impact how trust is computed. Clearly, this definition does not capture all possible elements of the trust context. Some elements are almost undefinable or unknowable except through proxies: the intentions of the trustor, their knowledge of the world and so on. These can be modeled through different proxies. Our emphasis in this brief has been on the elements of context that have been studied in social and cognitive psychology, and in computer science and engineering. These can serve as a starting point for introducing new modeling methodologies to trust context and trust models in particular. The framework is given as an outline in keeping with the survey nature of this brief. The next step is to define the appropriate formalisms to incorporate these modeling concerns into different interpretations of trust, and to test them in new applications through different means (Fig. 5.1).

Fig. 5.1 I trust you

References

1. D. Kahneman, *Thinking, Fast and Slow* (Farrar, Straus and Giroux, 2011, New York).
2. A.J. Perrin, K. Mcfarland, Social theory and public opinion. Annu. Rev. Soc. **37**(1), 87–107 (2011).